In loving memory of
Father Robert Voigt
Pastor, Healer, Friend

And for our children,

Mary, Joe, Ann, Paul, Margaret, Charlie,
John, Andy, Pat, and Clare,

somewhere behind the scenes in many of these letters.

SINCERELY YOURS

Letters from the Heart

Patricia Gits Opatz

To Marj –
Thanks for an old
friendship freshly renewed –

Sincerely Yours,

Pat

A Liturgical Press Book

 THE LITURGICAL PRESS
Collegeville, Minnesota

Cover design by Greg Becker

1   2   3   4   5   6   7   8   9

Library of Congress Cataloging-in-Publication Data

Opatz, Patricia Gits, 1928–
    Sincerely yours : letters from the heart / Patricia Gits Opatz.
        p.   cm.
    Includes bibliographical references (p.   ).
    ISBN 0-8146-2422-7
    1. Spiritual life–Catholic Church.   2. Imaginary letters.
   3. Catholic church–Doctrines.   4. Christian life–Catholic authors.
   5. Opatz, Patricia Gits, 1928–   . I. Title.
   BX2350.2.O64   1996   96-19518
   248.4'82–dc20   CIP

Contents

Introduction

LeMay Bechtold, Editor
The Liturgical Press
Collegeville, MN 56321

Dear LeMay,

It seems appropriate that this collection of letters should be introduced with a letter—and so I write to you.

It must be at least twelve years since you began suggesting that I should write a book of letters. Somehow, though, in all that time I couldn't quite put it together. In spite of your gentle urgings, no ideas came, nothing clicked. I continued to write the Sunday Bulletin commentaries for The Liturgical Press and many small pieces, but no book of letters. A few months ago something happened that gave me the push I must have been waiting for. I wouldn't tell this to just anybody, but I know you will understand.

Father Robert Voigt, to whom I dedicate this book, was a pastor and friend, as well as a fellow writer who frequently asked me to help edit his work. We used to read each other's creations to make suggestions, and he was always very encouraging about what I wrote. After he died last year, I thought of him often and recalled things he had said and written. At that very time I was having the uncomfortable feeling that I should be doing something further with my writing but couldn't quite settle on what it should be. A firm believer in the communion of saints, I asked Father Voigt one day if he would please give me a nudge in the right direction, as he might have done had he still been living.

Scene two: A few days later, Father's housekeeper, Louise Theisen, showed up at our back door with a book she said Ralph and I had given to Father Voigt back in 1978. She thought that we might like to have it now as a memento. I had totally forgotten that book, and if Father hadn't written inside that it was a gift from us, I would have thought that Louise was mistaken. The book is called *Illustrissimi*, a collection of letters written by Pope John Paul I.

The background is that the Pope, when he was still Cardinal Albino Luciani, had been asked by an Italian publication called *The Messenger of St. Anthony,* to write a series of letters to illustrious people, one each month. He agreed. The resulting letters are delightful—each one filled with humor and affection, while at the same time making a serious point. He tells gentle jokes on himself, shows his very approachable humanity, his wit, his humility. The letters are a wondrous blend of simplicity and erudition. They are addressed to people—living and dead, real and imaginary—as different as St. Paul and Pinocchio, Thérèse of Lisieux and Mark Twain, St. Francis de Sales and Charles Dickens.

After I had looked through the book and then read much of it, the idea began to hatch that, yes, I *could* do a book of letters. Mine will be vastly different from that gentle Pope's letters, of course, without the scope of his learning and holiness. Mine are from the perspective of a wife, mother, and grandmother (and various other roles), but my letters are as much from my heart and head as his were. Unlike the Pope, I have included questions for each letter at the end of the book for further thought or for group discussions. They often relate the subject to relevant passages in Scripture.

I believe that having the book of the Pope's letters delivered to my door was the nudge I had asked Father Voigt for—he returned the gift at just the right moment. I also believe that your inviting me all those times to do a book of letters played its part in the way it has all finally come together.

So, LeMay, my thanks to you, to Father Voigt, and to Pope John Paul I. In that illustrious group I also want to include Father Daniel Durken, who has given me encouragement over the years. By continuing to assign me those Sunday Bulletins, he has kept me close to the Scriptures and kept my mental gears from rusting. Not only that, but the letters from Bulletin readers around the country have given me the delightful surprise that people have actually enjoyed reading what I have written. For their encouragement I am also grateful.

Without Ralph, my husband and number-one fan and re-actor, this book would not have seen the light of day. To him goes my gratitude, always.

To St. Paul of Tarsus

On Letter Writing

Dear St. Paul,

It is no doubt presumptuous of me to be writing a letter to a bigger-than-life saint like you. Forgive me for saying so, but you have always seemed a bit intimidating to me. When I think of your brilliance, your knowledge of Scripture, your fierce zeal, your dramatic personal call from Christ, your missionary journeys over the known world, your divinely inspired writings still being studied and debated centuries later, your heroic life and death—well, you do seem quite remote and unapproachable. However, if I lay aside all those things and think of you as a writer of letters, then I am comfortable. I too am a letter writer. In fact, it is the subject of letter writing that prompted me to dare to write this letter to you. Maybe you will find my epistle a light change of pace from yours, maybe merely trivial. Nevertheless, I have decided to take the plunge.

Many years ago I made a New Year's resolution that whenever I thought of someone I had not seen for a long time, I would write that person a letter. I promised myself that I would not merely think of them and then forget it, but I would actually write and tell them how they happened to be in my thoughts.

Not long after that, as I was browsing in a bookstore, the name "Oletta Wald" caught my eye. Surely, I thought, there can't be more than one person with such an unusual name. Do you suppose that this woman could be the teacher I had in junior high school nearly thirty-five years ago? The Oletta Wald I knew had taught English and art; this Oletta Wald was the author of a book on Bible study called *The Joy of Discovery*. Here was my first challenge to keep that resolution.

I did. I wrote the letter and sent it to her publisher to be forwarded to her. (I also bought her book and read it.) I told Miss Wald that she had taught me more about grammar in the eighth grade than I had learned since, even as an English major in college. I recalled her pearly teeth and her wonderful art classes, in which I learned things I still remember about perspective and color. I specifically recalled a project for which we had to use primary colors and lettering to print a familiar maxim of some kind. From her list of suggestions I chose "He who does his best does well." (This was obviously in the days before enlightenment about exclusive language. It would not have occurred to me then to change it to "*She* who does *her* best does well," though she does!) There was one more thing. A fad in those days was to have friends write funny or romantic rhymes on the pastel pages of autograph books. We loved having Miss Wald sign ours because she always included a silhouette of a face, like the ones she did to illustrate children's books. I knew that all these details would sound pretty silly if *this* Oletta Wald was not *my* Oletta Wald, but I took a chance and mailed the letter.

I still have the answer I got in return; I brought it down from the attic just this morning. She *was* my Miss Wald, and she wrote, "Your letter warmed my heart on a cold March day." Whether she truly remembered me I don't know, but she said she did. She told me what she had been doing since those long-ago school days, creating a new career as a writer and presenter of Bible studies in the Lutheran Church. Well, Paul, I found that a lovely coincidence, because I do very similar things now myself. Rereading her letter today warmed my heart, just as my letter had warmed hers all those years ago. Letters are indeed wonderful things.

The same year in which I made that resolution I also came across a paper I had written years before as an assignment for a class in Dante. In that theme I wrote that long after I had forgotten all the other details about who was in purgatory or hell for what sin, I would remember one main lesson from Dante's

Divine Comedy—the importance of daily spiritual reading. No longer could I remember exactly where that lesson fit in. I knew it had been a powerful one, though, because even with a growing family of small children, I had been faithful to that daily practice. So, setting the paper aside, I wrote to Sister Mariella to tell her that I had thought of her and wanted to thank her for this good gift she had given me years before.

I had a beautiful response from her. But the beauty of it spread even further. Three years later I was in the hospital for major surgery and was running into serious problems. I still have the letters Sister Mariella wrote to me every single day for the first ten days of tough recuperation. One of them was especially powerful—a whole card filled over and over with a special version of the Jesus Prayer: "Lord Jesus Christ, healer of suffering, heal our dear Pat." I have since sent similar cards to friends who were very ill and in need of prayers. To write that prayer twenty or thirty times takes great concentration; your hand even starts getting sore, and you know that you are praying body and soul.

So you see, St. Paul, I have letter writing to thank for many good things.

Although these episodes brought joy to both sender and receiver, they were in themselves very small things. Your letters, on the other hand, are monumental. In fact, your writings make up a large part of our Christian Scriptures. Today we still read your epistles and, like your first readers, find news of your travels and hardships, along with instruction, encouragement, praise, scoldings, pleadings, exhortations, warnings, thanks, and powerful prayers. You wrote each letter to a specific group of Christians, with their own unique situation and problems. You gave them what they needed at the time, whether it was a boost, some clarification of a teaching, or a good scolding. (I'm certainly glad that I was not part of the congregation the day they read the letter in which you wrote, "You stupid Galatians!")

Sometimes I try to imagine sitting with the people when one of your letters arrived and hearing it read aloud. I hope you will pardon my saying so, but some of it must have been difficult to follow. You did tend to use long, complicated sentences that require some digging to comprehend. One commentator says that you "never attempted Attic elegance" and "deliberately avoided rhetoric," because you wanted people to be persuaded by the message itself and not by an elaborate style. He adds, "That is one reason why his grammar is sometimes wrong and his sentences unfinished . . . another is that he sometimes thought too fast or emotionally."[1] Somehow that fits the picture I have of you—passionate about your mission. How fortunate we are today to have the text right in front of us, so that we can examine your phrases, packed with theology as they are. One of the wonderful things about your letters is that though they were written nineteen centuries ago to very specific groups of people, they are also personal letters to us today—and meaningful in fresh new ways.

(It's true, there are many things in your letters that we still argue about, trying to figure exactly what you meant and whether you would say the same things if you were preaching today. Many women especially would like to ask you if you really would put the same strictures on them as you did in your first-century setting. In fact, you would find yourself as vigorously challenged as you were by some of those men in Corinth or Philippi. I hope you would agree with a statement of Pope John Paul I regarding your order that "women should keep silence in the churches." He wrote, "I believe St. Paul intended that prohibition to speak only for the women of Corinth and only for that given moment" because of a particular set of circumstances. He went on to note how many times you were comfortable about women prophesying in the churches.[2] This, however, will have to be the subject of a different letter another time.)

Did anyone ever answer the letters you wrote? I know from reading the Acts of the Apostles and some of your own writings that you experienced great discouragement at times. Did some of the people who had received your letters send you messages in return to cheer you in prison as we do today? Such a kindness would have been difficult in your day, of course, with no corner store to buy a ready-made card and so few people educated like you to read and write. Well, maybe you could consider this letter of mine one reply to your letters.

I want to mention two qualities of your letters that particularly appeal to me. One is the way you always include thanks. Time after time you begin a letter with such words as "I continually thank God for you," "I give thanks to my God every time I think of you," "We keep thanking God for all of you." What do you suppose would be the reaction today if a pastor, away on a business trip or vacation, would write his parishioners a letter telling them how thankful he was for them? Maybe they would actually grow into that gratitude and become the parish that the pastor is suggesting they already are.

The other thing in your letters that most impresses me is the powerful prayers you include. I especially appreciate the way they can be made into prayers as full of life and meaning for me today as they must have been for the people in your churches. What mother or father couldn't take what you wrote to the Ephesians and, changing a word or two, make it a prayer for their children: "May God grant them a spirit of wisdom and insight to know him clearly. May he enlighten their innermost vision that they may know the great hope to which he has called them"? Which of us couldn't benefit from your prayer for "perfect wisdom and spiritual insight"? And I love the way you pray that not only will your people grow to "understand" love better but will also "experience" it. As the psalmist says, we should "taste and see" the goodness of the Lord.

Do you remember the time you called the people *themselves* letters? It was in your second letter to friends at Corinth. You said, "You are a letter of Christ . . . written not with ink but by the Spirit of the living God . . . on tablets of flesh in the heart." I find that a fascinating idea—that each of us is a letter God has written to the world. In other places you urged your people to be "imitators" of God and of you. If you and God are letter writers and we are supposed to imitate you, then couldn't we do that by writing letters ourselves?

In this day of cordless and cellular telephones, answering machines, e-mail, fax machines, computer networks, and all the rest of our technology, some people have abandoned letter writing altogether. That's sad, because there really is no satisfactory electronic substitute for a personal letter. I frequently urge people to write letters because I know what pleasure they can be to receive. Often they react, "Oh sure, it's easy for you—you're a writer," or "Oh, I'm no good at writing." What they don't seem to understand is that it doesn't matter whether they can spell or find the perfect word or tell a great story. What does count is that they have the thought, take the time, and reach out person to person. Maybe it's all the better if there *are* a few misspellings or grammatical glitches—they simply make the other person feel comfortable about answering. A wise person once commented that we often fail to do the good because we insist on the perfect. That surely is true of letter writing. (If you, one of the world's great letter writers, often wrote flawed sentences, why should the rest of us feel self-conscious?)

One of the things you urge in letter after letter, Paul, is that if we are followers of Christ, then we must do loving things for one another, be of service to one another. Wouldn't you say that a good way to do that is to write letters? Whether it's a long personal letter, a short friendly note, a remembrance (like mine of Miss Wald), or a mere card saying "I thought of you today," it is a gift of kindness. To convince ourselves that such little things are important, all we have to do is remember how pleased we were the last time someone did it for us.

Throughout his teachings (and in yours too, Paul), Jesus commands his followers to do many things: seek reconciliation, offer forgiveness, show kindness, give alms. In the parable of the sheep and goats, people are examined on whether they fed the hungry, gave drink to the thirsty, comforted the sorrowing, visited the sick and imprisoned, or showed mercy. It doesn't take a great stretch of the imagination to see how many of these things can be done by letter.

Well, I have gone on too long, as enthusiastic letter writers often do. I thought you should know that your letters are nourishing and challenging people today just as they did when you first wrote them.

Thank you for writing,

Patricia Opatz

To My Mother, Blanche BaDour Gits

Cancer in a Different World

Dear Mother,

When I hear people complain about the world getting worse every day and bemoaning the passing of the "good old days," I think about you and me and breast cancer.

It is now thirty-nine years since you died of breast cancer. My world is as different from yours as it would be if you had lived in the Middle Ages. Your illness came at a time when nobody ever spoke the word "cancer" out loud. If it was referred to at all, probably only by doctors and nurses, it was "the big C" or "C-A." Nobody even said the word "breast." Except for being told your original diagnosis, it was never discussed. It was hidden away like something too shameful to talk about.

How could you bear the isolation of it? You must have felt like a leper in biblical times. True, you didn't have to cry out "Unclean," but the unwritten rule not to speak of it certainly could have made you *feel* unclean. Surely there must have been other women in Windom who had had mastectomies. Did you ever find out who they were or have a chance to talk with them about your experiences and feelings? If you did, you never spoke of it to me. And Dad told me later that you didn't even want him to look at you after the surgery, so ugly and mutilated did that radical mastectomy make you feel. When I think of the fear and pain you must have suffered—and alone—it breaks my heart.

Since then I've had my own bout with breast cancer, and it has been a totally different experience. Oh, there was still the shock of the diagnosis, the surgery (though not so radical and disfiguring as yours), the pain and the "intimations of mortality" to deal with. But there the similarity ends. These days people *talk* about cancer, even breast cancer, and praise God, we have support groups!

How I would love to take you with me to one of our monthly meetings. You would be amazed, probably even shocked, at how open we are with one another. At most of our meetings we don't have a formal program but simply talk. Each woman tells her story, starting with how long she has been a survivor. She brings us up to date on what has happened to her since the last meeting, how she is feeling, problems she has had to deal with, her emotions. So-called "boring" reports are the best; when a woman says she has had an "exciting" month, it means trouble. As the months go by, we get to know one another very well, and we have become a very caring community, like a family really.

Occasionally a surgeon or a physical therapist or an oncologist will speak to us. Usually, though, it's our own conversation that fills the hour, and it can go in some surprising directions. One night Jane told us that she had learned through Shirley about a woman in Romania who had had a radical mastectomy for breast cancer. There was no follow-up help for her, no prosthesis either, and she was having a hard time physically and emotionally. Jane offered to donate a prosthesis she no longer needed. It warmed our hearts the night some weeks later when Jane told us about the letter she had received from the Romanian woman, overflowing with thanks for this unique gift that had changed her whole outlook on life.

Two months ago Cheryl, a fair-skinned blonde, showed up with black curly hair and tan skin, the aftereffects of a year full of chemotherapy, bone marrow transplant, and more chemo. Her Swedish mother barely recognizes her; in fact, Cheryl hardly knows herself in the mirror. Some women have returned as surprised redheads, others with newly gray hair. When the new hair starts to grow, we celebrate and discuss ways to recycle used wigs.

Newcomers—and there are always some, what with breast cancer now touching one woman in eight at sometime during her life—get their questions answered, are reassured to see long-time survivors enjoying life, and are given hope and encouragement. Survivors (we do not call ourselves victims, as some newspapers do) are able to provide answers for new people who aren't even sure what questions to ask, the kinds of questions doctors can't anticipate. We exchange information about what our doctors have said, articles we have read, programs we have seen, anything that might be of help to another woman.

Mother, you would be amazed to see that we even *laugh* at these meetings—in fact, we laugh a lot! You had a wonderful sense of humor, but given the times you lived in, you couldn't have found anything very funny about cancer. We do. How could we not snicker at the "centerpiece" of prostheses at one meeting, there for the taking as other women no longer needed them? We exchange stories of weird-acting implants, mysterious reactions to chemotherapy and medications, the world of wigs, funny-sad accounts of people's insensitive remarks. Just last night we laughed over members trying to decide whether, given current statistics, it was worth it to invest in a $400 gold crown for a tooth or a new winter coat.

Humor comes from surprising directions. Sandy had us laughing one night with her argument that once a woman has had a mastectomy, she should get all subsequent mammograms for half-price. At one meeting, when our conversation ranged over edema, methatraxate, counting nodes, grades and bone scans, someone commented, "My, my, isn't it wonderful how educational cancer is—just look at how it has expanded our vocabulary." (I think all of this is called graveyard humor.) Someone else added that a few years ago she didn't even know what an oncologist was (and certainly not that "onc" is the Greek word for mass or tumor). We laughed again at the observation that when a patient buys green bananas, that's a good sign. Such laughter is possible only because we are there in numbers. I certainly wouldn't find anything humorous in any of it if I faced it alone as you did.

Humor and laughter as agents of healing—that's another old idea which has been rediscovered in my time but which you didn't have. Scripture speaks of it often, especially in the Book of Proverbs, and more and more studies support the idea with scientific evidence.

There are also times when we cry. Odd to say, perhaps, but women tell us that they feel comfortable crying in front of this group. We all have been in those same shoes and will understand. Now and then we have to face the fact of death, to grieve. Just last night we mourned the death of a beautiful woman who had been a member and friend.

One of the things I wonder about especially when I think of you is how you were able to face the periods of depression that so often accompany breast cancer. How I wish you had belonged to a group like ours, where you could have talked things through with other women who understood what you were going through, whom you could have phoned when you needed support, who would write to you when they knew you were feeling down—and pray for you.

I just checked an old dictionary, Mother, one from your era, and the word "holistic" is not in it (though I have read that it was coined in 1927). That's what you missed: the holistic approach. Nobody seemed to know about the intimate connection between your mind and emotions and what was happening to your body. Today there are volumes written about that body-mind connection. Studies show that our attitudes, beliefs, spirituality, laughter, and humor make a crucial difference in our ability to recover.

A recent newsletter from the Mayo Clinic cites statistics showing that breast-cancer patients who belong to support groups not only enjoy a better quality of life than non-members but also live longer. It seems to me that these statistics bear out in a scientific way what Christ meant when he spoke of two or three being gathered in his name. I believe he keeps that promise and sits in the circle with us at our monthly meetings. We have real pray-ers in our group, women who believe in the power of prayer and use it regularly. I wish you had enjoyed that kind of support.

There are kinds of prayer available to us today that you didn't have within your reach. For one thing, the Church's sacrament of the anointing of the sick, called "extreme unction" in your day, is much more accessible now than it was then. It is no longer reserved for the last hours on one's deathbed but can be received more frequently; we have a new understanding of its power to strengthen and heal. We also have healing services now, unheard of in your day, where we can be prayed for and blessed whenever we feel the need. We can belong to a prayer group, which will support us through illness, and we can call prayer lines for intercession. Names of the sick are read and prayed for regularly at Mass. Believe me, there is nothing secretive about it anymore—you really get prayers!

One kind of prayer radically different from what you were familiar with is one that I have found especially helpful as I dealt with cancer and four recurrences. It is called "faith imaging" or "visualizing." It is not really a new idea, for many of the great saints of old used imagination in prayer. Now, however, it is being used in new ways for healing. Praying in this way, we visualize our treatment and "see" ourselves getting well. Sometimes we picture Christ actively involved in our healing. This is one way of expressing the expectant faith that Jesus looked for in the people he healed, the kind of faith that so pleased him when he found it. Remember he said, "I tell you . . . everything you ask and pray for, believe that you have it already, and it will be yours." Visualizing our healing helps us to do this. It's like saying to God that we have such faith that we can already see the good thing happening.

Before I close, I want to tell you about two things that would have been absolutely unthinkable at the time you were facing cancer, events that I would love to have shared with you. At a recent support group meeting we sang some funny song parodies I had written about, yes, breast cancer. We sang, we winced, we laughed. You would have loved it. The other event took place last Mother's Day, when several thousand people gathered in Bloomington for a "Race for the Cure," and our family brought twenty members to join in the walks and the runs—your grandchildren and the great grandchildren you never met. You and I were both in their minds and hearts that day.

God is good. Since breast cancer took your life, we have come a long way, though goodness knows not far enough.

Someday we can discuss these matters and compare notes at leisure, though I hope you won't mind waiting a few more years for our reunion.

Until then, love,

Pat

To Audrey Mettel Fixmer[1]

On Friendship and God's Providence

Dear Audrey,

Our dining room table is spread thick with snapshots covering the early decades of our friendship, and I am looking family history square in the face. It wouldn't take a particularly clever historian to figure out from this display that our two families shared a lot of life during those years. You name it—picnics, Thanksgiving dinners, baptisms, birthdays, Christmas gatherings, swimming at Pelican Lake, snowy winter outings, emergencies when we took care of your children for a while or you took ours. Some simply show clusters of people gathered in each other's home for no special reason except that we liked each other.

And were they clusters! Some of those Thanksgiving pictures show as many as ten or fifteen children around the table—from just our two families, and there were still more coming that we didn't know about yet and were probably afraid even to contemplate. As those grown children now frequently ask us, how in the world did we manage?

One recurring theme (and I *do* mean recurring!) is the maternity clothes. Honestly, if I'm not wearing that dark black-watch plaid outfit, you are. We should have had that thing bronzed when we finally finished with it. And how about that brown plaid Pendleton jacket—well, pseudo-Pendleton—that was supposed to keep our secret a bit longer before having to tell our families we were pregnant again. That came just before the phase of hooking our skirt's waistband together with the biggest safety pin we could find. How thankful we were for those few years when "dusters" and chemises were fashionable. I have figured out that I was pregnant for a total of 8½ years. I guess it's the same for you. No wonder we avoided boxy-looking clothes for so long after that. Some woman once told me that it wasn't the smocks that gave us away, though; we looked "peaked" long before we got into maternity clothes. Thanks a lot.

Looking over these pictures reminded me of the hot summer day when I was poking around in the attic and found the packets of your letters that I had saved over the years. Some go back to your Holdingford and Melrose days, but most were taken after your move to Wisconsin, when we saw each other only once or twice a year. Maybe they are a partial answer to the question "How in the world did you manage?" The letters were therapy, companionship, confession, rage, frustration, delight, hope, comfort, celebration. The snapshots are only the tip of the iceberg of our history. The real story is in the letters. They, like the ones I wrote to you during that same period, were long—five, six, seven pages of single-spaced typing. And detailed! They were the kind of letters to delight the heart of a serious historian, for they vividly reveal the flavor and color of our daily lives. (And some odors too—this was decades before Pampers, and we lived with the perennial diaper pail in the bathroom.) You were separated from your family by several states, my mother was not well and I had no sisters, but we had each other and our letters. (We certainly did not indulge in anything as extravagant as long-distance phone calls.) Little did we realize that we were actually writing family history when we poured ourselves into those letters.

It's probably a good thing that the letters remained out of sight, so that I didn't find them for a few decades. Reading them too soon, when some of the wounds were still raw, might have been unbearably painful. By the time I brought them to you and we sat on your deck reading them, we had the healing of time on our side. Remember how we laughed and cried, the four of us, as we read about sick children, financial crises, fatigue and worry, changing jobs, repairing falling-down houses, unreliable cars, impatient creditors, bed-wetting, fighting, the annual pregnancy, breaking the news to our folks, unkind comments by neighbors, our love-hate relationship with the Church.

Of course, we shared the triumphant moments too—when the new baby was healthy and beautiful, one of our husbands got the prayed-for job, some long-standing bill was at last paid off, one of the children was finally catching on to toilet training, we had succeeded with some new project like bread-baking or needlework—and we counted our many blessings. We discussed favorite books, endearing things one of the children had said or done, and there were plans for the future. But the leitmotif of most of the letters is children and pregnancy.

It amazes me now to see that even as our nests kept getting more and more filled with chicks, all four of us kept busy in the outside world too, mostly with church organizations: Christian Mothers, Knights of Columbus, choirs, St. Benedict's Alumnae, your Daughters of Isabella, my Diocesan Council. Here and there will be a mention of some article you were writing or a talk I was working on, probably for the diocesan marriage preparation course. I can recall one panel on which we four appeared together, probably on the subject of marriage—we who were amateurs, muddling our way through, speaking as if we were experts. (That particular panel is the one I think of every time I come across the word "misled," because one of the panelists pronounced it "myzled." I'm not sure whether such oddities of memory make me a good historian or a bad one.)

Some of the events recorded in the letters and in diaries of the same period have become the stuff of family legend. One was the time both couples managed to find someone to take care of all the children and the four of us enjoyed a weekend vacation trip to Canada for only $15, our last twenty cents going for root beer on the final leg of the trip. With a trunk full of food, sleeping in a tent, washing our faces and changing clothes in gas stations, we even managed to afford one restaurant meal.

A routine luxury vacation would probably have been forgotten by now, but we won't forget that trip to Canada. For one thing, I was traveling with some residual bleeding since the birth of a baby three months earlier—and happily ignoring it so as not to be pregnant again immediately. You were regularly checking, becoming more and more certain that you were indeed already pregnant. Thus did Paul and Cathy enter the world—and wouldn't it be a bleaker place without them? Jesus tells us that a woman forgets the pain of childbirth in the joy of the new child, but I think it's the pregnancy she's happy to forget. When people talk about having only "wanted" children, they miss the point: there is a huge difference between a wanted child and a wanted pregnancy. Some of our pregnancies were not very welcome, but the baby was always a joy.

Also a part of family legend is the time your furnace broke down one January when it was forty below, and you and the children drove the forty miles to stay with us until it was repaired. Weren't there seven or eight youngsters between us then, the oldest probably eight? You and I sat up late that first night, cleverly planning activities and projects to keep the children happily busy all the next day; it was far too cold for them to be outside even for a few minutes. Weren't we creative! Unfortunately, by ten o'clock the next morning the children (obviously above average) had completed the projects, done all the activities, and wanted to know, "What can we do now?"

Some of the letters are brimming with plans—fabulous, life-changing, prosperity-guaranteeing plans. There was the water softener business our husbands were going to go into, encyclopedia sales, cosmetics, Tupperware, waterless cookware, the management track at J. C. Penney (starting pay $250 a month), rural mail delivery, and many other schemes and dreams. But God's plans for us included no get-rich-quick program. Progress came slowly, painstakingly, first in education, then in sales.

As the years went by and our families grew, as we became resigned to being exhausted most of the time, regularly exchanging maternity clothes, each month longer than the money, mini-epidemics of colds, flu, measles, and chicken pox going through the ranks, croup tents and tonsillectomies (we had three in the hospital at the same time one winter), we thought it would never end, we would never make it. But, wonder of wonders, it did and we did!

I said that our letters were part of the answer to how we managed; we know the other part of the answer is that we prayed—a lot. Our faith and our prayer carried us through every crisis, each crushing disappointment as well as each fear for the future. What would these children turn out to be? How would we ever hang on long enough to get them though school, past the perils of adolescence and into adulthood? We were sure that some would never make it; a couple would probably end up in jail.

But our faith paid off, didn't it? Looking back now, we can see God's guiding hand, and we can marvel at how well it turned out. Don't tell us that prayers don't get answered, that miracles don't happen! We are still with our husbands, enjoying married life more than ever; we didn't lose our wits, our humor, our figures (well, two out of three). And our kids did grow up. They not only stayed out of prison but became good, creative, contributing adults, women and men we are now delighted to have as friends.

Of course, it's easy to say that now. What the letters make clear is that in the middle of it, all we could see was the middle. There were no guarantees that it would work out happily at all. In fact, at times everything pointed to exactly the opposite. We "lived by faith and not by sight."

Do you know what we were really looking at that day on the deck as we read the letters? It seems too august and noble a name to give to such messy, daily matters, but I think it was the paschal mystery. The dying and rising of Christ—that's what it was all about. We were plunged into that mystery. It took place in us through countless little dyings and painful risings to begin again. Who would have guessed that we were involved in such important business?

Fortunately, during that plunge, prayer was an indispensable part of our lives, at home and at church. (Ah, yes, taking all those children to church—we could put together a substantial body of literature on that subject alone.) It's sad to think now that in all the praying we did, Scripture hardly figured at all. What little familiarity we had with the Bible came from one class we had had at school and what we heard at Mass. We knew the Bible stories, of course, but we had never been taught to apply Scripture to our lives, to pray it and make it active. The explosion of Scripture studies—discussion groups, books, study guides, commentaries, scriptural prayer books—all that came later. As a result, you and I didn't have the comfort that Scripture would have given us during some years of real testing. It's fascinating now, though, to find scores of Bible passages that fit exactly what we were living through day by day. It's as if they had been written with us in mind. Actually, they probably were—and for others like us. One place I frequently find that comfort is in the psalms. I wish that the psalms had been one of my mainstays in prayer then as they are now, but I recall having only a nodding acquaintance with them decades ago. Psalm 23, for example, has become familiar to us now through liturgical readings and hymns, but I suspect that we were strangers to it in the days of these letters. Think how many times it would have been a support, especially those lines

> Even though I walk through the dark valley, I fear no evil;
> for you are at my side with your rod and staff that give me
>   comfort.

I wish it had been one of our "by hearts" that day when you called to tell us that you had found your baby Gregory dead. We may not have known the term "paschal mystery," but you were surely plunged into it then. Recently I read in an old diary about that sad time:

> A terrible shock—I can't believe it yet. Bob and Audrey are all broken up. Ralph and I went to Melrose tonight. We put away Gregory's crib, changed the bedding on Bob and Audrey's bed, where he was lying when Audrey found him, and brought all his baby things home with us. The saddest part was that he was stiff when Audrey found him, and she can't get that ugly picture out of her mind. It's going to take a long time.

Talk about "walking through dark valleys"! (Do you ever ask Gregory to pray for your family or for one of his siblings having a problem? More than once I've asked our stillborn Elizabeth to pray for her brothers and sisters. I know she must take a very loving interest in them. This, too, is a rather new notion in my life, come to think of it, though it surely fits into the very old belief in the communion of saints. It's another thing I wish we had known then.)

I now have many psalm favorites that I could have put to good use in those early years with their dyings and risings. Think of the times our guilt might have been softened if we had reminded ourselves that "God knows how we are formed; he remembers that we are dust." We would often lie in bed at night feeling awful about the times that day we had been crabby, despite our morning resolutions to be cheerful and patient. (In a diary of that era, as I faced yet another round of toilet training, I wrote, "I'm promising myself not to make it a big issue this time, but to be content to walk softly and carry a big rag.") It would have helped if we had memorized those very concrete words about God knowing that we are, after all, dust. Perhaps it would have made us more understanding of the children and more forgiving of ourselves.

Think too how we could have used those reassuring words of Jesus that "fear is useless; what is needed is trust." I surely could have clung to those during a difficult delivery, when a croupy baby gasped for breath, or the time three-year-old Joe disappeared on his stroller and we found him a mile out of town heading for Hillman.

We might have snickered a bit thirty years ago to hear that numbers of children were "arrows in our quiver," as one of the psalms says. "Thorns in our side" was more like it on some days. But that picture came into clearer focus as the years went by and the children grew up. Now we truly do see them as "ammunition." We rely on their strength and loyalty. We see how they support us and one another. They are a kind of defense system for us now, aren't they, and a source of great pride and fun.

The paschal mystery—yes, that's what we saw as we read the old letters that day on the deck. We could look back and see that despite trouble and sorrow, frustration and disappointment, things had worked out well, far better than we had dared to hope. We learned through experience that what Scripture says is true: God is faithful and can bring good out of anything, provided we trust and have patience. We have seen with our own eyes this mystery that Scripture states in various ways:

"God makes all things work together for the good of those who love him."

"Only goodness and kindness follow me all the days of my life."

"All the paths of the Lord are kindness and constancy toward those who keep his covenant."

"Unless the grain of wheat falls to the earth and dies, it remains just a grain of wheat, but if it dies it produces much fruit."

Packets of letters from later decades would confirm this as tangled threads were smoothed out and obstacles we thought insurmountable gradually melted away. The paschal mystery, after all, is about rising, too, not just dying.

One of the ways we experienced the risings was probably in a sense of humor that seldom failed us. We did share a lot of laughs. People used to say that we had a special wavelength between us (like Brenda and Cobina) that would lead into funny wordplays, puns, silly songs, and skits. The never-failing psalms have references even to that. They speak of a "merry heart," a "glad heart."

In those pre-Scripture days I had never heard of Sirach, that wisdom writer from the Old Testament. Now when I hear him say, "A faithful friend is a sturdy shelter . . . beyond price . . . a life-saving remedy," how can I not think of you and those days when we all relied on each other for survival?

I think, too, of the beautiful line that says, "At nightfall weeping enters in, but with the dawn rejoicing." Popular wisdom says that we are now heading into the "sunset" of life, but in some ways I think we are now in the "dawn of rejoicing" phase. One of the benefits of this, of course, is that when difficult times come now, as they surely will, we will remember what we have learned, what God has already done for us, and we will not lose heart.

Reflecting on these old pictures and letters has been more than merely a sentimental walk down memory lane. I read once that there comes a time for each of us when we have to "take our life in our arms." That's what I have been able to do. Embracing the whole of my life now, I can see how blessed it has been. I am glad that you have shared so much of the journey with me.

With love to you and Bob,

Pat

To Today's Worried Parents

"All Manner of Thing Shall Be Well"

Dear Worried Parents,

Last Christmas at midnight Mass, my husband and I had the bad luck to sit behind a mother and her sullen adolescent son. There he sat hunched over, an undisguised sneer on his face, wearing his cap the entire time, and balking at every attempt his mother made to get him to sing or pray. He made it clear with every look and gesture that he felt aggrieved and put upon to have to be in this awful place doing this dumb stuff. I wasn't the only one who cheered silently when the usher came to their pew at Communion time and ordered in no uncertain terms, "Take off that cap! You're in church!" The boy did as he was told, but it was clear he felt that now he had an added reason to play the martyr. He gave his mother a sour look, sighed, sank even lower into the pew, and pushed his hands deeper into his pockets.

How I felt for that poor mother, and what memories were stirred up by the boy's performance! No doubt most parents of so-called baby boomers could relate their own experiences along similar lines. Some of you younger parents may be going through this period of child-rearing now. Well, don't despair—all is not lost. Those of us who came through the baby-boom wars may have some words of encouragement for you. And so I write this letter.

The baby-boom generation is defined as those children born between 1947 and 1961. The older ones of that group were going through their adolescence and high school years just as the effects of the Second Vatican Council and numerous other currents of change were beginning to sweep over us. They were about the age of the unhappy churchgoer we observed at that Christmas Mass. And family life became, as the kids used to say, "a whole nother thing!" (Do your youngsters still use that funny word "nother"?)

Years later, when they were adults, some of these children would tell us that they felt they had had "religion crammed down their throats" as they were growing up. We parents, who were convinced that the most valuable gift we could give our children was a grounding in their faith, were amazed at such an impression. When I first heard such sentiments, I was angry. But as the anger subsided, I began to wonder whether they had a point. *Did* we cram religion down their throats?

I have to admit that some of the things I did might be considered a bit hokey now ("noticeably contrived, artificial"). For one thing, there was the calligraphy I did in the hallway over the back door: "Unless the Lord build the house, they labor in vain who build it." It's a great thought, which I still believe, but what did visitors think, I wonder, when they saw that—and not in a convent but in a plain old house? Were the kids embarrassed?

If I had it to do over, I suppose I might also skip that Palm Sunday procession we had through the house, hanging palms in every room and talking about Christ being our King. Could the notion of Jesus as King have made much of an impression on youngsters between two and seven years old, especially in a country where we don't really know what a king is? Maybe they thought it was silly to hang all their baptismal certificates on the bulletin board on Easter Sunday, but it seemed like a good idea to me at the time. Our kitchen bulletin board was pretty liturgical, now that I think of it. And in one of the family slides we can clearly view the big headline MARY'S MONTH behind the May birthday child's head. Could all this have been a little too much?

There were some things we did that I think were good and wise, however, and I would recommend them to you parents now: that "God bless you" at bedtime with a small sign of the cross made on the forehead; rather chaotic attempts to pray the family rosary or any regular prayer routine; the Advent wreaths and songs; Saturday night rituals of shining shoes (and playing "tiger") and lining up prayer books and envelopes for Sunday Mass; prayers at meals and bedtime; religious art and spiritual reading material in the house.

Do you, like that long-suffering mother at Christmas Mass, sometimes sit with moody adolescents on Sunday morning? We did. You may have made the same disheartening discoveries we did: that one of the boys wasn't really going to church with his buddy as he said—they were meeting at the Dairy Bar and "hanging out" for an hour or so, then coming home at the appropriate time. Like us, you may overhear plans being made for camping trips or weekend visits, and Sunday Eucharist is not even brought up as part of the agenda.

Beleaguered parents of our day reacted in different ways to these distressing events. Some took the aggressive route. I know one mother who would actually call even her grown-up children and ask, "Are you being decent?" Some fathers would phone their adult children long distance on Sunday morning to ask whether they had been to Mass. The other school of thought included those parents who, afraid of "turning them off," just tiptoed around the subject with their offspring and hoped things would change. I think we probably belonged to the aggressive school at first ("As long as you put your feet under our dinner table, you go to church!") and gradually evolved into tiptoers.

One of the most maddening events for parents would be those special occasions when their adult children would come home for a visit, perhaps at Christmas or for some milestone wedding anniversary. Thinking they were doing Mom and Dad a big favor, they would go along to Mass. How those parents would sit hoping and praying: "O Lord, let this liturgy be impressive. Let this be one of Father's good homilies, not one of those rambling ones. Let it be fascinating and powerful, a magnet to draw these kids back. Don't let the choir be ragged and embarrassing, as they often are. Let it be one of their better Sundays." As often as not, however, the children remained unimpressed, unmoved.

Then I would be angry with myself for sitting there tensely, waiting for flaws to explain away. It wasn't fair! Here were these young adults (like other people who attend Mass only once or twice a year) making judgments based on very little evidence. While they might see the pastor in the pulpit giving a lame homily on one particular Sunday morning, we saw more. Our picture included his regular visits to the hospital to visit parishioners, his kindness toward grieving families, his simple lifestyle, his hospitality and openness to new ideas, his powerful prayers and blessings. So this "mediocre" homily would come across to us as part of a whole loving person whose life we shared year-round, not as a speech that we were there to evaluate or find entertaining. (For all I know, our children were not making these judgments at all. I might have simply imagined that they were, so sensitive were we to the possibilities of the moment.)

Parents couldn't help but speculate that if these children belonged to a parish and joined in its activities, it would make a difference. If they came to know the pastor and worked with him, got acquainted with the people and shared in the life of the community, *and* contributed their own considerable talents, then they would hear with the ears of their hearts. The homily would speak to them personally. These were our negative moments, but we found much that was positive too.

As the years went by and parents adjusted to the indifference of their baby boomers, we were given encouragement from many sides. Our pastors told us to pray for our children and set as good an example as we could. I recall the advice of a visiting priest who was conducting a parish renewal: "Pray and be glad if your children have a good spiritual life of any kind—leave it to the Lord to choose the direction they will go." After all, whose children, whose sheep, are these people anyway? Though we love them dearly, think of how infinitely more God loves them. Why should we let ourselves worry about them excessively?

How can we not take heart when we see these children turning out to be wonderful adults and exemplary parents? True, it is hard to see them being indifferent toward what has always been the central focus of *our* lives. It is always tempting to taunt, "Well, all that religion couldn't have been *too* bad—look how great *you* turned out!" They often express admiration for our good marriage and family life but can't seem to get the idea that there is a connection between those good things and our faith and prayer life.

Parents are admonished in many ways to let go of their children; this particular letting go may be the hardest of all. Perhaps you ask yourself the kind of questions my husband did at that time: After nearly a thousand years of Catholic Christian heritage on both sides, back through Poland and Belgium and Ireland, is it all going to end with this generation? Will we have to content ourselves with a "remnant" like the Jewish people after the Exile—four or five out of ten?

Let's look at this in a more optimistic light: Couldn't this be a perfect way of testing that very faith that is at issue? I mean, if we really believe what we say—that God loves us, journeys with us, is concerned about all the events of our lives—well, then, of course God lives in *our children* too with that same loving concern. They will find God through their own struggles, just as we did. Surely God can work better if we don't try to hang on to the controls.

So I write this letter to encourage you parents who are still struggling to try to take the long view and not make premature predictions. Look for the good in your children and encourage it. Keep communication lines open and always do the loving thing, no matter how tempted you may be to judge harshly. Remember how much power there is in prayer. (We are reminded on her feast every year that St. Monica prayed for eighteen years for the conversion of her son Augustine. Eighteen years—big deal! That's nothing compared with how long some boomer parents have been praying.)

Most of us are familiar with Elisabeth Kübler-Ross's analysis of the stages a dying person goes through: denial, anger, bargaining, depression, and finally acceptance. Bishop Robert Morneau adds one final stage to that list for the dying person: anticipation or expectation. If our faith is what we proclaim it to be, there should be at least the beginnings of a happy anticipation, maybe even a healthy curiosity, about what lies ahead after death. Can you see a parallel between those stages and what we parents go through with our children? Let's not lose heart but look with happy expectation at what our daughters and sons will turn out to be. If we place them in God's hands, not only will something good happen, but very likely it will happen in a manner totally different from, and much more creative than, the scenario *we* had in mind.

When you are discouraged or worried about your children's religious life, remind yourself of what the mystic Julian of Norwich wrote centuries ago. Anthony de Mello called them "some of the loveliest and most consoling words ever written."[1] Julian wrote: "Sin is behovely [that is, evil is inevitable] but all shall be well, and all shall be well, and all manner of thing shall be well."

With prayers for your kids and ours,

Pat Opatz

To Pope St. Gregory the Great

Of Words and Music

Dear Pope Gregory,

How amazed you would be if you could see what has become of the famous Gregorian chant named for you! I think you would be pleased, and I know you would marvel at God's mysterious ways. I write this letter not only to tell you about what has happened but also to ask you a question.

I realize that scholars generally agree now that chant did not actually start with you, though it was long assumed that it did. Actually its origins are very obscure. It may have developed in the eighth or ninth century in the Carolingian Empire (now a part of what we call Germany) and not with you two centuries earlier. Perhaps you were given the credit because of your well-known interest in serious music and also your efforts to bring some definite order into the liturgical works of your day. (I recently saw an imaginative drawing from the thirteenth century that actually shows you composing a chant, accompanied by King David playing the organ!)

One commentary suggests that attaching your name to chant might have been a "Carolingian publicity technique" for advertising purposes.[1] Well, whoever ran the ad campaign in the ninth century would have to be mightily impressed by the publicity which that same chant is getting today. I am sure that you would be interested in hearing about the latest adventures of this chant called by your name for centuries. That is what I want to tell you about before I ask my question. Thus my first letter ever to a pope.

After what seemed to some people to be a total eclipse of Gregorian chant after the Second Vatican Council, except for special liturgies and sacred concerts, it has come back in the most unexpected way—as pop music on CDs. CD stands for "compact disc," something you could hardly have dreamed of back in the sixth and seventh centuries, or to quote St. Paul, what has happened to this ancient music is "far more than you could ask or imagine."

It began in Spain at the Abbey of Santo Domingo de Silos, the home of Benedictine monks just like you. Some enterprising men recorded the monks as they sang the ancient chants, produced the sounds on a compact disc, and began to promote it. At first it was a surprise hit only in Spain; then it spread like wildfire worldwide to become the fastest-selling classical record in history. After only months it had sales of 2.2 million copies and is still going strong. Others, seeing the success of it, began to copy the idea, recording other groups singing those beautiful sacred melodies. Just recently I counted more than twenty-five different CDs of Gregorian chant for sale at a local store. Reports tell us that the music is purchased and listened to mostly by young people aged sixteen to twenty-five. They often use the word "transported" to describe how they feel when they listen to it.

(You will be comforted, St. Gregory, to know that the royalties from the recordings will go to the needy in many countries and for overdue monastery repairs. Your fellow Benedictine, the abbot of Santo Domingo, reacting to all the publicity, said, "We are simply monks who sing to pray better.")

Imagine my wonderment the other day when I saw Gregorian chant advertised in a catalog under the heading "New Age Music." That may sound to you like something out of the Scriptures—the Book of Revelation perhaps. This new age is something very different, however, a mix of ideas and practices some of which you might find objectionable. Still, here it is advertising "your" chant and selling these recordings in vast numbers in many parts of the world—parts of the world you not only didn't see but would not have heard of.

Gregorian chant was a part of my life, too, especially during my four years at the College of St. Benedict in St. Joseph,

Minnesota. Early every Thursday morning we would meet with Sister Urban, a dedicated Benedictine nun determined to meld our ragged student voices into a smooth-flowing sound to match the schola of sisters who sang from the balcony. Grabbing our veils, we'd race through the cloister walk and gather in the chapel before class to rehearse the appropriate chants for the coming Sunday's Mass. We didn't always enjoy crowding that session into our busy lives. Nor did we appreciate Sister's patient efforts—or our results—at the time. However, those lovely sounds gradually soaked into our bones and found a sympathetic home deep in our hearts. We came to love them. What I'm wondering is this, Pope Gregory: Do you think that this holy osmosis could happen again today?

I find myself thinking about the young people who are listening to the newly popular chant today. Do they hear the words and wonder what those flowing Latin lines are saying? Will they soak up the lyrics to this music as they do their other popular hits? I try to picture a teenager, dressed in regulation jeans, gold-loop earring, Nikes, baggy knit shirt, and baseball cap, singing "Ubi caritas et amor, Deus ibi est"! Might he eventually come to *believe* that "wherever there is love, there is God"?

Or what about the yuppie (there's another concept you have to imagine), man or woman, tooling along the freeway on the way to the office, playing the chant on the car's CD player. Will the words of the *Gloria* prompt them to look out of the window and observe that indeed "heaven and earth *are* full of God's glory"?

The possibilities are endless. I like to imagine it being piped into elevators and offices; that would be much more humane than what we hear there now. Suppose that while we sat in the dentist's chair or doctor's waiting room, we were soothed with words from the *Agnus Dei*. Might it actually "grant us the peace" it prays for? Instead of being inflicted with monotonous pop music while we are put on hold during a phone call, what would happen if we heard a version of the *Salve Regina* instead? Do you think it might put us in touch with Mary, "Mother of mercy"? If people were to hear "Veni, Sancte Spiritus" over and over in the background as they rode the elevator, wouldn't it have to make a difference in what happened in their business meetings and relationships? I mean, wouldn't the Holy Spirit actually *come?* Who knows, perhaps a comeback of the *Dies Irae* heard on a car radio would even keep drivers on the alert. What a concept! "Awesome!" as that teen listener might say.

The American poet Maya Angelou believes that words do have this kind of power. She says:

> I am convinced that words are things, and we simply don't have the machinery to measure what they are. I believe that words are tangible things, not ephemeral . . . that words, once said, do not die. . . .

She goes on even more specifically, as only a poet can:

> I do believe that words hang somehow in the draperies and settle in the upholstery and help to polish the furniture, go into the clothes—really—and then go into the body, as effect. So they cause us to be well and hopeful and happy and high-energy and funny and cheerful. Or they can cause us to be depressed. They get into the body and cause us to be sullen and sour and depressed and, finally, sick.[2]

If this is true of words in general, how much more true it must be of God's word. Do you think that this word power works even when it has to be translated from Latin into one's own tongue? I tend to believe it does. Every day we learn more about what an amazing instrument the Creator has fashioned in the human mind. Consider the startling thing scientists are telling us now, that the mind is not just in our brain but in every cell of our body. Put that together with the power of words, and surely something wonderful could happen.

Many of the words used in chant are, after all, God's word as found in Scripture. I think of what we are told about the impact of that word: James compares it to a seed that is planted in our hearts and grows to produce fruit. Isaiah assures us that it is never sent out in vain but always accomplishes its purpose. And you know those powerful words from the Letter to the Hebrews that call God's word "living and effective, sharper than any two-edged sword. It penetrates and divides soul and spirit, joints and marrow; it judges the reflections and thoughts of the heart." Now that's word power!

Just imagine what could happen to the people listening today to the word of God in Gregorian chant. After being planted, the words would begin to sprout and bear fruit, the fruit of the Spirit—such things as peace, love, patience, gentleness. Heaven knows our poor suffering world could use a bumper crop of such produce. Some people decry what they consider the atheistic aspects of New Age practices—not without some reason, I suppose. Some of their writings fail to take into account evil and suffering and our need for a Savior. Still, who knows, maybe God (who is, after all, *very* creative) is using this most unexpected means to get back into young people's lives and hearts. It wouldn't be the first time God used a side door to slip in unnoticed.

Well, I just thought you would like to hear the latest on the chant that bears your name and the potential it has for continuing to do good. Dear Gregory, please join me in praying that the people who buy and listen to those recordings will be touched to the heart by the powerful words. Pray that the love of God will penetrate their "soul and spirit, joints and marrow," and draw them closer to the God who created both them and the music.

Cum cantu in corde,

Patricia Opatz

To W. Timothy Gallwey

On Being Here Now

Dear Mr. Gallwey:

A couple of our grandchildren who were visiting yesterday noticed your book on my shelf and laughed. They couldn't quite visualize me reading a book on the subject of tennis. Actually, I can't blame them. They had good reason. You see, Mr. Gallwey, I have never been noted for my athletic ability. All through grade and high school, I was usually one of the last ones left on the bench when they chose up teams—unless, of course, it was for a debating team or a speech contest. The only sport in which I ever excelled is one that nobody today seems to have heard of and is probably extinct by now: deck tennis.

In my day there were few organized sports for girls, but gym classes were more than enough to satisfy me. The occasional unit on folk dancing was more to my liking. Would you believe that I fell and broke my arm playing basketball in one of those classes in my sophomore year? People swore that there wasn't a soul anywhere near me, but I never believed a word of it.

Despite this unlikely athletic background, I do have your book *Inner Tennis: Playing the Game*[1] on my shelf. This is the third time I've borrowed it from one of our sons. I confess I skip over the passages about the actual playing of the game and focus instead on the underlying ideas. The way you teach tennis—as an *inner* game—it can be a metaphor for anything. You have convinced me that the inner skills you teach your tennis students can be applied to all of life's lessons.

"Tennis as metaphor"—I like that. You use it often to stress one of your key lessons: the importance of *staying in the present moment*. You demonstrate that being totally aware of the present is essential for playing good tennis and equally important for living a conscious life. The fact that this kind of mindfulness has been practiced and taught by sages from every culture confirms your belief, though you may be the first to apply it to tennis.

The wise person who expressed that idea best for me, however, was neither sage nor guru. He was a small grandson who wanted to describe something that had disappeared, but he didn't know the word, so he said, "It just 'peared away!" (To get the right effect, you have to pronounce it "peeeered away," preferably with appropriate gestures.) It's a colorful and accurate way to describe what happens when we wander out of the present moment. If we are anxious about what may happen tomorrow or brooding over what happened yesterday, we aren't here today. Our minds and emotions have strayed into the past or into the future. Since we can't truly *be* in the past or future, though, we have "just 'peared away." We aren't anywhere.

Reading your book has made me aware of the many ways in which this disappearing happens, and painfully aware of how often it happens to *me*. It's clear from your book's dedication, Mr. Gallwey, that your insights on inner tennis have come by way of wise teachers from the East. It's a pleasure to read and learn from them. Finding confirmation of that same wisdom in my own Scriptures has been important for me. It has moved me to try ways of applying principles of inner tennis to my life, especially the idea of *presence*.

This strange "'pearing away" from the present can take funny forms. I have been in homes, for example, where there are wall-to-wall scatter rugs covering the carpeting, saving it for some unknown future, I suppose. It's the same mentality that keeps slipcovers on furniture and plastic on lampshades long after the departure of any children who might have soiled them. I think, too, of households where the "good" dishes are kept in the china cabinet, unused year in and year out.

A nineties way of escaping the moment is the ever-present headset. It seems to be standard gear for every walker, biker, and runner, as basic as the correct shoes and shorts. What are these people listening to, I sometimes wonder. A Spanish lesson, one of the great books, motivational lectures, music—a vigorous march, perhaps, that helps them maintain their pace? Judging by their distant gaze, whatever they're hearing has taken them "far, far away, elsewhere" as my mother used to say. I wonder how many of the sights and sounds around them they actually experience. Much as I admire their discipline and endurance, I must say they do look as if they have "'peared away" completely.

By far the most extreme case of this I have seen was in a film about "the first computer nomad," a man who built himself a computerized recumbent bike that is basically self-sustaining. Attached to the handlebars is a fully equipped computer with monitor and keyboard run by solar power. The computer console puts out a signal that is picked up by ultrasonic sensors in the helmet, so the driver can control the cursor by simply nodding his head where he wants it to be. Thus, he writes as he pedals. A built-in cassette recorder is also part of his equipment, so he can record as he goes. Not only that, he has a solid-state refrigerator that can create fifty units of cold from excess solar power. This device also creates power by pulling heat out of his body with a heat exchanger on his helmet, which in addition has a rear-view mirror, lights, microphone, and other devices I couldn't even identify. It must be great fun. Still, I like to think that he turns off all the gizmos to enjoy and appreciate what he sees around him before he begins to tape or type. With all of his gear in action, just where *is* he present anyway?

One of the ways you teach the lesson of presence is by playing a game you call "I've never met my wife before."[2] You don't mean treating your wife indifferently but rather listening carefully to what she says, hearing only the words, setting aside all previous feelings about her, both negative and positive.

You recall the time your wife offered you a critical suggestion that normally would have provoked some bristling rebuttal on your part. This time you chose not to let past episodes influence you, not to arouse your usual defenses. Putting all preconceptions aside, you heard only the words themselves, clear and unencumbered, as if spoken by a stranger. Because you were fully present in the moment, you listened to *her* instead of your thoughts *about* her. You said that the experience was a revelation, because when you heard the naked words, you heard the truth about yourself. You commented, "It was something I really needed to be told, but heretofore I hadn't let myself hear it from my wife."[3]

Another way you teach that lesson is by telling your students to "see the actual." You want them to apply this to the movement of a tennis ball, but it fits other things in life too. Often we look at a situation or a person, and instead of seeing what is actually there, we see a version already fixed in our minds. It may be a remembered emotion or a fearful preview of the future. Either way, it distorts what is present and actual.

Any time we hear ourselves wishing away our lives, we can be sure that we have "'peared away" and are no longer fully present. A song popular some years ago said it well: "Life is what happens while you're busy making other plans." I suppose we've all done that: dreamed of some wonderful day in the future when we can start *really* living. "When the kids are all through school." "When the mortgage is paid off." "After this one last class." "After I lose fifteen pounds." But we never quite reach that day; there is always one more bit of living to get out of the way first. Our attitude is like that of another old song: "We'll have good times by and by next fall when the work's all done." It's hard not to fall into that trap; here's where I've found the Scriptures helpful.

A good antidote for that attitude can be found in Psalm 118: "This is the day the Lord has made; let us be glad and rejoice in it." Those of us who find ourselves pulled into the past or future could use this line as a morning prayer, emphasizing the first word: *This* is the day—the only one we have. It's a gift in our hands right now, but we will never know what potential it contains unless we stay present to it as it unfolds.

Knowing that worry about tomorrow is the villain that often tempts us away from the present, Jesus addresses it explicitly: "Don't worry about tomorrow. Let tomorrow take care of itself. Today has troubles enough of its own." I wonder what our days would look like if we actually did let tomorrow take care of itself. We could still make our plans and appointments, write our lists, do the necessary preparations; but then we would have to let go and with total trust turn the results over to God. Jesus knows our weakness well, though, so he reinforces that lesson time after time, telling people not to be afraid, not to be worried or let their hearts be troubled. In a particularly tender passage he says:

> Are not two sparrows sold for next to nothing? Yet not a single sparrow falls to the ground without your Father's consent. As for you, every hair of your head has been counted; so do not be afraid of anything. You are worth more than a whole flock of sparrows (Matthew10:31).

Thinking about this passage made me curious. I went back to a journal I kept ten years ago to see what I had been concerned about. It's true, the things that worried me then and kept me awake nights had all smoothed out. Some of them were not even remembered; were it not for the journal, I'd have forgotten them completely. The child away at school and miserable with homesickness has finished college and earned a master's degree; a talk I had agreed to do and was dreading has long since slipped from memory; children whose lifestyles concerned me have become devoted spouses and parents; deadlines, meetings, assignments, and health problems that were on my mind then have been forgotten. Seeing that evidence in my very own handwriting was powerful testimony to the truth of Jesus' words about worry. Yet I'm afraid that a look at this year's journal would show another menu of worries, just an updated version of those recorded ten years ago. Maybe I and other journal keepers should read parts of our old journals regularly. Reviewing the difficulties of years ago, now overcome and left behind, might lighten our hearts and make us more trusting of today.

Worry isn't the only symptom of deserting the present moment. Even more common is the bad habit of not listening, something that both you and Jesus speak about. The person mindful of the present moment is a person who listens well, as you did, Mr. Gallwey, the day you heard your wife's words so clearly. Jesus was often troubled by people who listened but didn't hear or understand, looked but didn't see. He pleaded, "Let him who has ears to hear me, hear! . . . Listen carefully to what you hear." That kind of seeing and hearing requires that we stay firmly in the present. It means seeing the actual.

One of the easiest and least expensive courtesies one person can offer another is wholehearted listening, where we get out of our own heads and walk with the other person's thoughts as best we can. There are times when all we need for healing or comfort is for someone to listen to us in that total way. This was proven dramatically in a listening exercise I once read about and never forgot: two people listen to each other for twenty minutes. While one speaks, the other is silent, makes no response by word or gesture or facial expression but gives full attention to the person speaking. Then they reverse and the speaker becomes the listener. The results are amazing. The speakers find it enlightening and healing to be listened to with such complete attention. They express unexpected thoughts, surprise themselves with revelations, see themselves with new insight, arrive at answers hidden until then. Such total presence has been transforming for both parties.

There are less dramatic ways of being present. For several years my husband and I were part of a Yokefellows group who joined inmates at the local prison two evenings a month. At these gatherings we would pray together, study a Scripture lesson and see how it fit our lives, share our stories, and get to know one another. There were times we went home feeling frustrated because the discussion had not gone well, and we thought the evening had been a failure. Time and time again the chaplains would assure us that the gift of our *presence* was the most important thing we brought to the meetings, not the success of the lesson. Inmates, who were often bitter about the world outside, were touched by volunteers' willingness to be present with them and hear them. We have no way of measuring the blessings that flow from those moments when we give the gift of total presence to another person.

Being present in the now is prescribed these days as a way to avoid anxiety and stress. "Be here now," we are told. "Do what you are doing." "Live a conscious life." "Practice mindfulness." "Stay awake!" (That one is from Jesus.) Thinking of those statements brought to mind an article I read many years ago in which a woman commented that the best thing about housework is that it's so boring. While one is ironing or washing or cleaning, she wrote, one's mind can take off and play with ideas, plans, creative projects. I found that notion quite appealing at the time and often mentioned it to other women who, like me, were engaged in housework and child care full-time. Now, however, as I learn about the value of mindfulness, I think that the writer might have been mistaken.

Since then I have come to understand how beneficial it is, mentally and physically, to be present even to the routine daily things, to do them all consciously. A friend once told me of being served a cup of coffee by Brother David Steindl-Rast, a Benedictine monk who practices mindfulness in many ways. She said his total presence to that simple task gave her the feeling that this was the world's most important cup of coffee and she was the most important person ever to be served. I wonder if this is related to what St. Benedict says in his Rule, that the "utensils and goods of the monastery" should be treated "as sacred vessels of the altar." Think of applying that to the tools we use in our kitchens, our gardens, our offices. Such an attitude would surely bring us into mindfulness. You say something similar, Mr. Gallwey, when you write, "In daily life, I find that I have always been most satisfied when I exert my energy fully on whatever I am doing, no matter how unimportant it may seem."[4]

Probably the most forceful teaching Jesus gives on the subject of presence is not in his words but in his actions with others. We see repeatedly in the Gospels that when people demand or beg for his attention, he makes himself wholly present to them. Even when they interrupt his travels or his rest, sometimes rudely, he focuses on them and responds; he listens and answers.

One such moment comes shortly after Jesus has learned that John the Baptist has been killed, and he wants to go off by himself for a while. He must have been shaken as well as saddened, wondering what John's death would mean for his own future. He invites his disciples to go with him to a secluded place. But a "vast crowd" gets there first; there they are, waiting for him when he arrives. What happens next amazes me: Jesus doesn't get back into the boat and escape out to sea, doesn't run for a hiding place in the hills, doesn't tell the people to go back home or even wait for a little while. He pities them, spends the whole day talking to them, and even feeds them. Only after all that does he take time to be by himself. I don't know about you, Mr. Gallwey, but when I think of the way I handle interruptions, the way I covet my private time, the way I react to people who intrude on my tidy schedule, well, I'm awestruck by the way Jesus meets the demand of total presence. He probably would have been a great tennis player.

There is another Gospel episode, quite mysterious, that shows the contrast between seeing what is actual and missing the whole point. Jesus is at a dinner party when a woman comes in with a jar of precious perfumed nard. She breaks the jar and begins pouring the perfume on Jesus' head. The other guests react "indignantly," are "infuriated," complaining that the nard could have been sold and the money given to the poor. Jesus not only defends her action but says that the story of it will be told in her memory for as long as his own story is told. Apparently Jesus and the woman, unembarrassed, are the only ones at the dinner who "see the actual." The other guests hear only their own prejudiced thoughts about the woman and her extravagant gesture.

Would you agree, Mr. Gallwey, that it isn't possible to be perfectly mindful every moment, that there are times when we really must hurry and do several things at once? For those hectic periods we're advised to practice one thing a day with total presence. (Maybe a good place to start would be not eating meals in front of the TV.) Whenever I have worked at doing something wholly in the present, I have observed three things happening:

First of all, I slow down. It's impossible to remain wholly present in the moment while trying to do several things at once. Mindfulness requires putting the brakes on long enough to concentrate on one thing at a time. I've begun to notice how often I rush through things even when there is really no hurry. I attack chores as if all the children were still home and this house was the beehive it used to be. (This habit from the past affects my husband in a different way: when he buys groceries, he comes home with five-gallon and ten-pound sizes of things as if there were still twelve of us around the table three times a day.)

When I deliberately slow my pace and look only at the present project, I find out what it means to be peaceful. I get a more accurate view of what is going on in my life. Recently I was struck by a Thai saying I heard: "Life is so short, we must slow down." That's the exact opposite of the usual "wisdom," that because life is so short we've got to hurry. I have found it valuable to think about this other view, and I see the truth of it.

Something else happens when I slow down: I discover myself becoming quiet. Giving one's full attention to the activity at hand automatically stills the talkative mind—and mouth. Quietude (isn't that a great word?) makes it easier to be aware of God's presence in ourselves and all around us. Centering prayer done faithfully is an especially good way of experiencing the richness of this slowing and quieting. In this prayer we practice making ourselves present to God's Presence within us.

A third discovery I've made when I am mindful and see things as they are is that I can't help being thankful. More and more it becomes clear to me that everything in my life, including my life itself, is a gift. When we are mindful, we begin to see the beauty in the smallest things. We see how extraordinary even the ordinary is. What an amazing, totally undeserved blessing *everything* is!

Whether these qualities can be applied to the game of tennis, Mr. Gallwey, I'm not sure. To me, the slowing and quieting suggest a player's concentration, and thankfulness suggests the joy of playing well. (Who knows, even I might have been an athlete had I known all this years ago.)

I trust you don't mind my using your book in this unorthodox way, Mr. Gallwey. Though I will almost certainly never play the game, I can make good use of tennis as metaphor. (If it's any consolation to you, our sons who have read your book *do* play tennis and play it very well.) Especially satisfying for me has been finding your lessons on staying in the present moment echoed in the teachings of the Scriptures.

I will end my letter with one version of this lesson that is enjoying widespread popularity lately. It has been reproduced on greeting and prayer cards, books, and posters, in magazines, and even on T-shirts. The first time I saw it was as a poster on the door of the prison chaplain's office. I wouldn't be surprised if it might even have some practical application to a good game of tennis:

> I was regretting the past
> and fearing the future.
> Suddenly my Lord was speaking:
>
> "My name is I Am."
> He paused. I waited.
> He continued,
> "When you live in the past
> with its mistakes and regrets,
> it is hard. I am not there.
> My name is not I WAS.
>
> When you live in the future
> with its problems and fears,
> it is hard. I am not there.
> My name is not I WILL BE.
>
> When you live in this moment,
> it is not hard. I am here.
> My name is I AM.
>
> —Helen Mallicoat

With thanks here and now,

Pat Opatz

To Father S. E. Mulcahy

God's Gracious Gift of Imagination

Dear Father Mulcahy,

This is both a thank-you and an apology, prompted by finding your letter yesterday in an attic box labeled "Memorabilia." (Yes, even though you have since gone home to God, I expect you to get the message—one of the benefits of faith.) When I was a school girl and you were our pastor, one of your duties was to teach our release-time religion classes. You moved on to another parish after a few years, and I had no reason to think I'd ever get another lesson from you. We never saw each other again. But your letter forty-plus years later gave me something I treasure as much as any lesson learned in that armory basement classroom across from Windom High School.

When I discovered that you were in a retirement home, still alive and active ten years ago, I decided to write you a note. I just wanted to say hello and mention a few happy memories you might enjoy. I wrote about things that I thought might help you to remember me, though I understood that was unlikely. It had been many years, after all; you had been in other parishes and met hundreds of people since I was part of your flock.

I reminisced about painting the background for the Christmas crib scene at St. Francis Xavier's, a night sky with Bethlehem in the distance. That was fairly successful, but the paint job you asked me to do on the Last Supper carved into the altar front—that was a different matter. Remembering those intense reds, blues, and greens, I was relieved that the church had since been demolished and replaced with a new one.

I hesitated about sending you a book I had recently written because I thought you might find parts of it a little bizarre. You must be well into your eighties, I speculated, and my chapters about mental visualization, imaging, and finding an inner guide might be offensive to you, or at least bewildering. (Ha, little did I know!) I decided to take the risk and send it anyway.

This is where the apology comes in, Father. You will forgive me, I hope, for thinking that just because you were old, you would be lackluster, weak-minded, or unimaginative. Now that I am ten years closer to eighty myself, I know that to be a vicious lie! I was soon to learn that lesson firsthand.

Your answer came in March, six pages handwritten. You remembered me, along with a number of small events I had forgotten. I didn't recall ever helping you with the parish bulletins, impressing you with my typing skills, or once getting some ink on myself from the messy duplicating machine. Your remembering was a great compliment; even more welcome was your response to my ideas on imagination: "And your book, Pat. I would like to put seven very strong adjectives together to tell you how precious it is for me. I've read it twice, and each time it's newer." That was a pleasure to hear, but the best part came next:

> I have my own thing going since my Seminary Days, 1926-1930, when Latin was the language of the Church. I would go to the library every Saturday P.M. and read the old Church Fathers of the first century of martyrs and I got so I could talk to them and also the Apostles. For example, John was the youngest Apostle. At the Last Supper he loved our Lord. He leaned over and put his head on the Lord's shoulder. We talked together. "Oh John do that again. I want to love Jesus the way you do it." I got the martyrs to talk to me about how they overcame fears—weakness—even martyrdom, and especially weakness of Faith. [This way of praying] has been part of God's power and grace in my life.

Wow! And I was worried you wouldn't get it! Receiving your affirmation was important to me. I think it freed me to try other ways of using fantasy in prayer myself. I'm not sure why I initially felt so uncertain about it. After all, great saints of the past did the very same thing. I believe it was Teresa of Avila, one of the most often quoted authorities on prayer, who said that her mind was so scattered that she *had* to use imagination when she prayed. More recently I was reassured by the words of Morton Kelsey, who writes that imagination is "one way of experiencing reality—and meeting the divine Lover."[1]

All these ideas were bubbling away recently when I was asked to give a talk on the subject of prayer to a group of busy women. They were finding it hard to fit prayer into their lives because of being pulled in too many directions day and night. It was not just the younger women either, busy with careers and families; even from older women I frequently heard the lament: "Honestly, since we retired, it seems we're busier than ever!" I decided I would talk about ways in which even the trivial stuff of overcrowded days can be starters for prayer, provided we use God's gifts of imagination and humor. (With that in mind, I decided to call the talk "Waste Not, Want Not.") Here was an opportunity to pass along the lesson your letter taught me. I'm afraid my ideas on using imagination won't sound as reverent as yours, Father, but they're all kitchen-tested. If they work for me, I thought, these busy women might also find them useful. Experts say that all good teaching is storytelling, so I would simply tell them my stories.

Several years ago I read that after the death of a very holy sister, the members of her community discovered in her journals profound spiritual insights and wonderful prayers. It was very impressive. I confess, though, that it also gave me a good laugh, because I knew what people would find if they went digging for spiritual treasure in *my* journals. You see, Father, one of the ways I have used imagination is to "baptize" totally unrelated things and make prayers of them. I think of them as code words that only God and I understand.

Take, for example, my Clint Eastwood Prayer. You probably never heard of stony-faced Clint, but he is well known today. In one of his films he deliberately provoked people until they went for their guns, because then he had an excuse to shoot them dead. In a menacing voice he egged them on, "Go ahead, make my day." That sounded to me like a very good morning prayer: "Go ahead, Lord, make my day." It says that I am putting the day in God's hands and will do my best to accept it all gracefully. Events later in the day, both good and bad, often remind me of that morning offering.

It's more likely that you would recall an early TV show called "This Is Your Life," another of my code words. It calls to mind passages from Paul's letters, where he says, "I live now, not I, but Christ lives in me" and also "My life is hidden now in Christ." Our faith teaches that we don't simply live a *changed* life but actually live *Christ's* life. We can call that truth to mind every morning by praying, "Lord, this is *your* life." Whether the day goes well or falls apart, we know that we aren't facing it alone. Actually, the two sayings together might work even better: "This is your life, Lord. Go ahead and make my day."

If you ever saw reruns of the old TV show "Hogan's Heroes," you have heard my Sergeant Schulz prayer. Schulz, the comic German guard in a prisoner-of-war camp, wanted to make no waves. If the prisoners were digging tunnels or planning escapes or building bombs, he didn't want to know anything about it. Time after time he would say passionately, "I see nothing. I know nothing. I understand nothing!" Don't you think that at times that is a good prayer too? Situations arise when it expresses our relationship with God exactly, because when you come right down to it, we really don't know much—much is mystery. "We walk by faith and not by sight." (But not you—*now* you walk by sight!)

You see what I mean, Father Mulcahy—this is not the sort of inspiring message found in saints' journals, but I have the feeling that you would approve anyway. Among the printed materials you sent me was a brochure giving all the details of a week-long Caribbean cruise you had planned for your fellow residents of St. Ann's Hospice—all by way of imagination, of course. Nobody actually left the building. Evidently you had nourished your imagination all those years and still enjoyed using it.

One of my "waste not, want not" ideas is more suitable for a women's group than for you, Father, and I hope you won't find it in bad taste. (I suspect that in the next life we won't be squeamish anymore about mentioning perfectly normal physical things.) In those old parish days, I doubt that either of us had heard of the "hot flash," something peculiar to women of a certain age. I call the hot flash the "burning bush syndrome"—on fire but not consumed, like Moses' bush in the desert. If it's going to happen anyway, I figure, why not take advantage of it? Why not use it as a reminder of God's indwelling presence, which at that moment is felt physically, potently, head to toe. I suppose I wouldn't honor it with the name "sacramental," but it certainly acts as an effective sign of an interior reality. A real attention-getter.

We can also use imagination to post signs and reminders. Others won't know what they mean or even notice them, but for us they can be signals, little nudges to make us aware that God is always present. One of mine is related to bridal wreath bushes.

Five years ago I was at the lowest ebb of my life, in the hospital and certain that I was heading into my final illness. One of the skills we patients were taught there was to use imaging, to visualize ourselves being well and accomplishing our life goals. "Life goals" sounds grand, as if these had to be significant life achievements. Not mine. The two goals I visualized were hanging clothes on the line to dry on a breezy spring day and seeing the bridal wreath in full bloom again. I've hung wash on the line many times since then and have seen the bridal wreath blossom four summers in a row. Last June I took a close-up picture of several branches in full bloom. I keep that snapshot in a book I read every morning; it reminds me of the way God saw me through some terrible days and gives me an unmistakable message of hope.

My use of imagination isn't always so "off the wall," Father, but much more conventional. For one thing, I think it takes a good imagination to read the Bible well. God has filled the Scriptures with images so rich that we really must picture them with our mind's eye in order to soak up their full meaning. We shortchange ourselves if we don't take the time to use our imagination, visualizing in detail what God suggests in images. Prayers far more knowledgeable than I say the same thing. I especially like what Morton Kelsey writes about Thomas Merton: "He noted that imagination can discover real meanings, not just produce distractions and delusions, and he stressed reading the Bible imaginatively, both as a way of exercising imagination and also to find the full meaning contained in the Bible."[2]

One reading highlighted for me by imagination was Jesus' invitation: "Come to me, all you who are weary and find life burdensome, and I will refresh you. Take my yoke upon your shoulders and learn from me, for I am gentle and humble of heart" (Matthew11:28-29). I had never seen a real yoke in action, but I knew what they were. I had seen pictures of two oxen held close together with a huge wooden yoke laid across their shoulders, and around each head and neck a hoop of metal or leather. With this yoke and all the right straps and reins, the farmer could make the oxen carry massive loads and do heavy work. For the oxen, then, a yoke meant being forced to submit to someone, to yield and allow someone else to make the decisions, give the orders, be boss.

Picturing such a yoke makes Jesus' words sound very strange. Who would willingly accept an invitation to take on such a burden? What could we possibly learn bent under a yoke? Why not try it and see?

In my mind's eye, I put myself under such a yoke with Jesus for a partner. I couldn't see much of anything except the ground—and Jesus' feet next to mine. I could watch every step he took, how fast and in what direction, what he avoided and stepped around, when he stopped and started. I could see that a smart yokemate would try to follow that pattern step for step. It was painfully clear how much distress one stubborn ox could cause by struggling to go its own way, faster or slower, in a different direction, maybe balking completely. Such a partner would be a pain in the neck for both.

Bent under that yoke, I also experienced how well each of us could hear the other. Bound close, always in each other's presence, we could pick up even the quietest sounds, every word, even every breath of our partner. We could communicate constantly.

Such imaging made the lesson clearer, I think, than if I had merely thought about the passage. Sharing Jesus' yoke so vividly, I could see how we need to adjust our steps to his, listen to his words, stay constantly in touch, and avoid being the stubborn ox that tries to go off on a tangent of our own. Thus we really do learn from him and his yoke and get some of that promised refreshment.

An unexpected bonus of this exercise was the new layer of meaning that certain Scripture passages took on. Jesus' invitation to "follow me" sounds very different when you hear it under a yoke. "Take up your *yoke* and follow after me" gives a new twist to the old words. "Let us keep our eyes fixed on Jesus" makes me see again the feet of Jesus trudging under the yoke. Even some Old Testament words take on new depth when we imagine Jesus' speaking them:

> I will instruct you and show you the way you should walk;
> I will counsel you, keeping my eye on you" (Psalm 32:8).

I have noticed, Father, that once such pictures have been created in the mind, they surface readily when the same passage is read again. They become a resource we wouldn't have if we hadn't used our imagination, a mental library we can draw from. (Or would we call it a "resource center," as they do now?)

A modern writer you would have appreciated, I'm sure, is Anthony de Mello, who uses imagination in the service of prayer just as you did. In his book *Sadhana,* for example, he provides specific instructions for numerous prayers using fantasy. One of my favorites is the one in which you imagine yourself sitting high above a great city at the end of the day as the lights come on. A holy person well known in the area approaches you and says gently, "If you go down to the city tonight you will find God." Some easy guidelines follow to help you imagine your trip down into the city and what you find there. You are encouraged to leave your mind open and not think that there are places you "ought" to go.[3]

I believe I was a shade skeptical when I first tried this, but I became a believer when I saw that it really "works." To my surprise, I really did find Christ in the city—once in a church, once in a park with old people watching children play, and once in a library. We "talked" for awhile (very *quietly* in the library), and I came away each time with some new insights and a feeling of refreshment. That must be what you experienced on those long-ago Saturday afternoons in the seminary library.

Why do you suppose we were never taught as children to pray using imagination? The saints had done it. You were praying that way as a young seminarian. Why did no one tell the rest of us that it was easy and natural and fruitful? How did you get started? Did someone teach you, or did you learn by reading the saints' lives and experimenting on your own? I wish you had surprised us by teaching this in one of our religion classes, but I suspect that never even occurred to you—too human? too physical? too unorthodox? (Too bad!) It's a very personal way to pray; maybe that's why you hesitated to pass it on, especially to unpredictable teens. We had probably been told to meditate on the mysteries in the life of Christ when we prayed the rosary—that took imagination. So did the stations of the cross, but I don't recall being taught other ways to use fantasy in prayer.

What do you suppose would have been the reaction if one Sunday back in the forties you had given a sermon teaching the congregation ways to pray with the imagination, maybe even leading them through one for firsthand experience? Can you imagine (of course you can) what some upset parishioners would have said about it over Sunday dinner? I know that some worshipers in church that day would have taken in the lesson like cool rain on parched earth and treasured it all their days.

On second thought, maybe there wouldn't have been much table talk. For some people it would have been a topic far too intimate to speak of openly; they'd be squirming in church and would be too embarrassed to talk about it afterward. People didn't discuss such matters then as we do now. Parish groups didn't meet to pray or study Scripture or tell their faith stories. More likely we discussed Church history or local parish matters. I guess you did the prudent thing in not sharing your secret, but it was our loss.

Maybe you got the idea for imaginative prayer from reading the Gospels, from Christ himself. What a creative imagination he must have had to dream up stories and characters like the prodigal son and his brother, the good Samaritan and his fellow travelers, the rich man with his full barns. It takes imagination to look at a mustard seed, a pearl, a bowl of dough, a dragnet and see the kingdom of heaven; to look at flowers and think of King Solomon; to see a log in a person's eye. And how about those "whitewashed tombs, beautiful on the outside but inside full of filth and dead men's bones"? They certainly came from a colorful imagination.

The brief note of thanks and apology I started out to write seems to have grown all by itself into this long letter. Judging from what you wrote, though, I think you must enjoy exchanging such stories. Writing it has been a boon to me, convincing me all over again how imagination can strengthen and deepen one's faith. Surely it is one of the more delightful ways we are made in the Creator's image. De Mello calls fantasy "an untapped source of power and life,"[4] almost the exact words you used in your letter.

Do you know another lesson I learned from your letter? How little we know about what really goes on in another person's head and heart. My parents were your parishioners for years, and Dad was a trustee, but your meetings, I'm sure, were about furnace repairs or fund–raisers, not about nourishing the spirit. How could your parishioners have suspected what a rich inner life you had? It makes me wonder what additional lessons you might have taught us about prayer.

Morton Kelsey writes that "in order to reach the deepest levels of relationship to God, one has to put imagination to work and start upon the daring venture of seeking . . . God."[5] That's what you were doing, and I am grateful that you shared with me a bit of your daring venture. Better late than never!

Your old friend and student,

Pat Gits (Opatz)

To Absent Catholic Baby Boomers

An Invitation to Take Another Look

Dear Catholic Baby Boomers Who Have Left the Church:

You were on my mind one recent Sunday morning in church—yes, all of you. It wasn't the first time, certainly, but it was an especially memorable one for me. That was the morning when the realization began to sink in that I really was facing another recurrence of cancer. I went to Mass feeling a combination of terror and depression, to think that I would have to go through all that awful business again. It was exactly the right place to be, however: the ancient rituals and prayers, the familiar hymns, the reading of the timeless words of Scripture, the homily on the faithfulness of God's love, people all around me believing and praying—I felt powerfully held and sheltered. I was very grateful to belong to that group, stretching down through the centuries from the very time of Christ. I felt the security of being among people who believe in the power of prayer and put it into action for others in need.

That's when I thought of you. It is always at such times that I most regret that so many of your generation have turned their backs on all this. I wondered, What in the world will *they* do, who will *they* turn to if they find themselves in my situation? I hope and pray they will not be bereft but will come back for sustenance and support.

It's your parents who make up my generation (we never got a special title for ourselves as you did, even though we're the ones who provided the boom). But now you are the adults and parents yourselves, and we have moved further along into life.

From here we look back and wonder about your generation and the one to follow you, our grandchildren. We wonder especially about your inner life, your deepest beliefs, if and how you pray, what you are teaching your children about God and "the things that really matter," to quote St. Paul.

You might be surprised to hear how often you and your spiritual lives come up in the conversation of your elders. At meetings, over coffee, on the phone, at class reunions, perfect strangers who discover that they are of the same vintage can soon be exchanging stories about their boomer offspring and their religious practices, or lack of them.

Some of these worried parents take the confrontational approach. They might ask (just before the son or daughter heads for the airport is a good time), "If you should die unexpectedly, what kind of funeral would you like—and where?" knowing full well they haven't been inside a church since their wedding day. This is apparently calculated to shock the recalcitrant ones into some serious soul searching.

The secretive approach is taken by other worried parents. In this group is the grandmother who furtively baptizes the new baby in the kitchen sink when she goes to help out after the birth. Questionable, but understandable. These sly ones also send anonymous gifts of religious magazines to children who have dropped out, in the hope that something will rub off on them or catch their eye.

Some parents are inventory takers. They check through their children's magazine and book collections, finding publications on gourmet cooking, home decorating, the arts and science, health and child rearing, psychology and fitness, but nothing dealing with religion, Christian spirituality, or Scripture. These parents also take note that although their sons and daughters are regularly getting advanced degrees or attending workshops and seminars in their professional field, their last class in religion was in the eighth or tenth grade.

Other worriers are the elderly parents or grandparents who are seriously concerned that their sons and daughters won't be familiar with the custom of praying and offering Masses for a loved one who has died. "Who will pray for me?"

they worry. Fortunately, Mother Church prays for all those who have died "in the hope of rising again" at every Mass as well as at special times throughout the year. Still, these parents miss the comfort of knowing that their children will remember them not just in fond recollections and photo albums but in prayer.

I confess that a similar thought occurs to me when I recall family vigils around the bed of a dying parent or a close relative. I remember the rosaries we prayed together, a ritual that was comforting to the dying person and equally consoling to the gathered family. Now parents wonder, "Will my children gather around *my* deathbed and see *me* off with prayers? Do they know how to pray a rosary as they did when they were little? Do you think they might have a prayer book or use the psalms?" Perhaps this is one of the things parents should discuss with their children—not just the will and the power of attorney but who will pray for them.

It seems that we are not the only ones interested in your spiritual life. Not long ago a national news magazine featured a cover story about your "Search for the Sacred." According to the article, your whole generation is now engaged in a spiritual quest. It states that "there are spiritual seekers of all ages, but baby boomers are at the head of the march." Apparently you are the particular focus of these studies because it was your generation more than any other that threw off the religious influence of family and upbringing. "For baby boomers in particular," says one account, "spirituality was off the radarscope. Instead, as a generation, boomers embraced political activism, careerism, even marathon running, with an almost religious zeal. But it's suddenly OK, even chic, to use the S words—soul, sacred, spiritual, sin."[1]

A professor of religion at one university says that as boomers get into their forties, they are forced to accept the truth that "neither jogging nor liposuction nor all the brown rice in China can keep them young forever."

Apparently the searchers among you are taking a very eclectic approach and shopping for meaning in a wide variety of places. We read accounts of people "into" Buddhism, especially Zen, crystals, pyramids, channeling, New Age practices, native

American spirituality, yoga, angels, meditation in diverse forms, and everything in between.

It isn't that we think you are all great sinners in need of conversion—nothing like that at all. In fact, we think you have turned out to be fine adults; we are proud of what you have done with your lives. So this is not one of those scolding, fire-and-brimstone, "Why don't you go to church?" letters. There will be no theological arguments or proofs from me. Faith doesn't come by way of argument anyway but is more a matter of "Taste and see." My reason for writing is simply to say this: As you look around for a spirituality to answer your deepest needs, please include on your shopping list the Church you left. You may discover that in many ways it is not the same as you remember it. You may also find that you have been missing out on some beautiful things it has to offer you and your children. I hope you will also find that, especially in some of its most ancient traditions and rites, it has all that the other paths offer, and more besides.

I suppose all of us parents are secretly hoping that our children will follow the route of one man in that magazine article. His plans were to take the "usual college-career" path, but he dropped out when he came near death following surgery. Studying under a Zen master, he meditated and learned practices that helped him find the sacred in the events of daily life. Ultimately, he "discovered he could also find truth in a place he had long abandoned, the Roman Catholic Church. He found new inspiration in studying the mystics and the saints."

One thing you have to say for the Catholic Church—it's always "there" for you, as it was for this man. It's something you can complain about, rail against, find fault with, tell stories about, ignore or despise, but no matter how angry you may be with its weaknesses, it goes on offering its comforts and consolations. It still preaches the gospel, celebrates God's nearness to us, and does enormous works of charity. Like most good mothers, it is usually trying to reform itself and be better. Despite its faults, it has the wisdom of ages to recommend it. In its history are versions of all the good things so many are now seeking. I suspect that the Church you are angry with is the institutional side, but it has another side too—it is also the people, the Body of Christ, and the rich, centuries-old tradition handed down through them.

I like to think of the Church as a vast house of prayer, circling the globe and reaching into the remotest corners. Every minute of every hour of every day and night, there is unceasing prayer of all kinds connecting us to one another and "making God and his redeeming love present in the world."[2] Prayer rises from contemplative men and women in hermitages and monasteries, from ordinary people beginning their day's work with a quiet hour, from others meditating and praying with the Scriptures, from the youngest children to the very oldest grandparents. There are prayers of praise and joy, of grief and need, from every land and language.

Think of just the Eucharist. There is not an hour when it is not being offered somewhere in the world—in magnificent cathedrals, parish churches, ghetto missions, army barracks, and hospitals. In every single one of those Masses, you and I are remembered and prayed for. People you and I will never know are offering prayers that fill our needs, as ours fill theirs. I see that worldwide mesh of prayer like a hum rising from the surface of the earth. It calls to mind a line from "God's Grandeur" by Gerard Manley Hopkins: ". . . the Holy [Spirit] over the bent world broods with warm breast and with ah! bright wings."

It was that sense of solidarity with the praying body of the Church that was such a comfort to me on the Sunday morning when I thought about you. That is what I don't want you to miss. I hope you will give your old home Church another look, set aside any grievances you may have, and try again to "taste and see" how good it can be.

Hopefully,

Pat Opatz

To the Third Servant

A Parable and Murphy's Law

Dear Sir:

Storytellers often base their characters on real people they have known. I wonder if that's what Jesus did when he introduced you in the parable of the silver pieces (also called the parable of the talents). Your character there is so recognizable, so much like people I know (including myself sometimes), I suspect that Jesus must have met you or someone like you in person. He didn't give you a name, so for centuries you have been known simply as one of the anonymous servants given sums of money to invest for your master. You're the one always analyzed and discussed, though, because of the way you took your silver pieces and buried them in the ground. Based on that strange behavior, I've recently taken the liberty of calling you Murphy. It's an unlikely name for a man of first-century Palestine, I admit, but I have my reasons.

You see, where I come from, we have a humorous maxim which states that "whatever can possibly go wrong, will go wrong." It is known as "Murphy's Law." When I read your explanation for burying instead of investing your portion, I recognized Murphy's Law at work. Forgive me for saying so, but you are really a perfect embodiment of it. (I dare to insult you in this way only because I confess I'm sometimes a Murphy myself.)

When your master asked for an accounting, you said, "My lord, I knew you were a hard man. You reap where you did not sow and gather where you did not scatter, so out of fear I went off and buried your thousand silver pieces in the ground. Here

is your money back." How you must have cowered when he
called you a "worthless, lazy lout" and threw you out.

I think he was wrong, though. It wasn't laziness that made
you act as you did. To me it looks like Murphy's Law at work
in your imagination: you felt in your bones that if anything
could possibly go wrong—and you could think of dozens of possibilities—that's just what would happen. You knew your boss to
be hard and demanding, so your imagination went to work creating disasters. Numerous failures came to mind: if you invested
the money here, someone would cheat you out of it; if you
bought a piece of property there, you'd never find a buyer ready
to take it off your hands; if you put it in the bank, you just *knew*
the bank would fail or be robbed. No matter what you did, it
was going to end up with your master in a rage and you losing
your job. You never once entertained the possibility that a plan
of yours could succeed. That's Murphy's Law all right.

How different it must have been for your fellow servants.
I picture them rushing home that night filled with excitement,
eager to tell their families, thinking to themselves, "What a
deal!" Their imaginations went to work too, not creating potential disasters as yours did, but having fun playing around with
ideas, brainstorming, researching, asking questions, searching
out good advice, making lists, figuring numbers, praying for
guidance. When they finally decided where their portion of the
money would earn the best profit, they took the plunge.

Think of how good they must have felt about themselves afterwards, what a boost it was to their self-confidence. The master
observed this in them and rewarded it. But poor Murphy, you
were probably more scared than ever, afraid to make a move. I
was reminded of you the other day by a poster I saw in a hospital room. Pictured was a small sailboat far out on the ocean. At
the top was the word RISK, and under the picture, "You will
never discover new oceans unless you have the courage to lose
sight of the shore." That's you, Murphy, and me too sometimes.

What kinds of sermons, if any, you heard in your syna-
gogue, I don't know. Maybe you were exhorted, just as we are
today, to "be open." I have heard dozens of talks on how important it is to be open: to the Word of God, to the promptings

of the Holy Spirit, to grace, to God's love, to the needs of others, to change and growth. We hear it on all sides. Be open—it sounds simple and easy enough. I have a sneaking suspicion, though, that if it's simple and easy, we're not doing it right. I hate to say so, Murphy, but I suspect that God expects us to live dangerously.

I have heard various applications of your story over the years, but this is the one I find most appealing: God can do great things in our lives only if we are willing to open up and take some risks. I remember a speaker making that point once when he was asked, "Why is it that some people experience God's action so dramatically in their lives, almost miraculously, while others' spiritual lives are pretty humdrum?" He answered that some people take the risk of actually believing what God says and acting on it. Their lives are more exciting because they leave some loose ends, make room for God to come in and act. In other words, they don't insist on having all the answers or getting ironclad guarantees.

I don't know if that rings a bell with you, Murphy, but I suspect that your mind works the way mine often does. I say that I want God's will to be done, but deep inside I'd feel safer if I could write the script myself. Open-ended plots are too risky, too unpredictable. Besides, God uses very bumpy, hazardous paths to get to the happy ending. In fact, things often get worse before they get better. That's the trouble with living dangerously—it's dangerous.

Yet, God's promises are so personal and loving that we are foolish not to accept and trust them. The poet Maya Angelou pictures her Momma as one who did. A true believer, she was also explicit. She took God's words to heart and let God know that she was depending on them. Faced with a crisis or problem, she would pull herself up to her full six feet, look up to the heavens, and proclaim firmly and forcefully "to her family in particular and the world in general, 'I will step out on the word of God. I will step out on the word of God.'"[1] What a model for the Murphys of this world!

Just think of the many times, for instance, Jesus tells us not to be afraid, not to be anxious, not to worry, not to let our hearts be troubled. (It's a message his Father had also sent many times, in Isaiah and the psalms, for example.) Do you know what I noticed in the Bible one day, Murphy? After many of those "Do not be afraids" there is an exclamation point. Isn't that interesting? It looks to me as if Jesus' original words against fear were so emphatic that the only way they could be translated accurately was with exclamation points. We might be surprised to hear the tone of voice and see the body language Jesus used when he said, "Do not be afraid!" Must have packed quite a punch.

I'm learning that part of the bargain when we take a chance on God is that we have to be hospitable to the new and unexpected. In fact, I believe the saddest part of your story is that by ruling out the risk, you also ruled out the possibility for mystery. There was no way for God to put any surprise into your life; you were shut up tight. It was as if you buried yourself in the hole with the coins and pulled the hole in after you. The irony is that because you left no room for God's providence, you ended up with precisely what you had tried so hard to avoid: the master's wrath and the loss of your position. God needs room to maneuver.

Often God maneuvers and beckons us toward challenge and growth by bringing new people into our lives. Each one gives us a fresh opportunity to learn, because every person comes with life experiences unlike those of anyone else who has ever lived. With each one we cross over into a whole new world, then return to our own world enlarged and changed in some way.

Murphy, have you ever asked yourself "What if?" What if you had taken the leap of faith, invested the money and made even a modest profit? You probably would have been praised and promoted like the others. It could have changed your life forever, written you an entirely different future. I sympathize with you, though, because I know it's hard to live with uncertainty.

I'm wondering if the problem is that we think of God the way you thought of your master—hard and unyielding, incapable of understanding our weakness, waiting for a chance to nab us in some fault. It doesn't sound much like a loving Father, does it? Sometimes I think we must be myopic when it comes to the scriptural passages clearly showing God as compassionate, endlessly forgiving, eager to bear our burdens, worthy of trust.

I have to admit, Murphy, that sometimes when we trust, we do trip and fall, end up with egg on our face, or, like Peter on the water, start out strong and then start to sink. I suppose that's what you were afraid of. Don't you think, though, that if we keep trying, eventually we come to realize that even in our worst failures, we are still in God's hand, that it's safe to wait and trust?

I'm kind of embarrassed as I reread this letter, because I know that I haven't been fair. Here I am lecturing you about shutting yourself off in fear, yet I do the very same thing. At least you were concerned about a major decision, whereas I "sweat the small stuff," to quote a popular T-shirt. Would you believe, for example, that I have a chronic case of "phone-a-phobia"? I actually wince when a phone call is for me and have to steel myself to make a call; I consider the phone an instrument of torture. I frequently bargain with my husband, "I'll write the letters if you make the phone calls." When I first heard of a *cordless* phone that could go with you *everywhere*, I thought it sounded positively demonic. You'd think I had been stalked by a homicidal maniac or been the object of threatening calls, but I haven't. For some people it's bats or mice; for me it's phones. Just one more of life's little mysteries. But you can see what I mean about shutting out divine surprises. It's a small matter, true, but definitely points to a streak of Murphy in me. I need help as much as you do.

There are places in the Gospels where Jesus is portrayed as "astonished" or "amazed" by someone's total trust. I suspect that he still enjoys being astonished now and then. Why don't we try to astonish him, Murphy? I'm game if you are. Let's try to be more open to the new and unexpected. As a motto for all of us Murphys, I am going to suggest a line from Psalm 82, where God says, "Open wide your mouth, and I will fill it." What a challenge and what a promise that suggests! I think I'll try to answer the phone with a smile from now on and make two difficult phone calls every day. Well, one for sure.

Here's to living dangerously,

Pat Opatz

To Barbara Brown[1]

The Demon of Depression

Dear Barbara,

We're almost up to the Fourth of July again, and as always when this date rolls around, I think of you. I don't suppose I will ever again pass this holiday on the calendar without recalling the one we spent together in the hospital's mental health unit. How ironic to observe Independence Day while suffering from depression, a disease that makes one about as UN-independent as it's possible to be.

I remember vividly how we were all herded down the hall that night to the solarium, where there would be a good view of the fireworks, looking for all the world like school kids out on a field trip. I was pushed along in my special recliner-on-wheels and was imprisoned in it for what seemed like hours, waiting and waiting for the show to start, then waiting and praying for it to end. Crowded into that room also were patients from the other, locked end of the Unit. Some were young people in for drug problems or attempted suicide. I wonder where those two girls are now who sat in front of me joking loudly and boldly about how they were going to "bust out." They were funny and heartbreaking at the same time. Did you, like me, find yourself thinking, "How in the world did I end up here?" ("What's a nice girl like you doing in a place like this?") I suspect that everyone in that room felt the same dismay.

That feeling was never more intense than the day I made my first visit to the required occupational therapy class. Closing

71

my eyes, I can see myself again in that large bright room amid other patients diligently working on their projects. My first task was to select something to work on from a bewildering array of projects available. I took the first thing I saw—it really didn't matter. It turned out to be a ceramic plaque of the so-called Serenity Prayer, the kind I'm told that graces the wall at every AA meeting in the country. There I sat in my wheelchair, painting noble words about serenity, tears flowing down my cheeks, listening through a headset to a talk on depression by Earnie Larsen. I recall saying to myself, "This cannot be me, not Pat Opatz, not in the occupational therapy room of the hospital's mental health unit painting a ceramic plaque!" But it was. It was definitely me.

My husband still wears the woven leather belt I finally finished after I got home, but to this day I cannot get myself to hang up the little "Welcome" cross-stitch piece I did. It's buried in the back of a filing cabinet drawer, where I run across it occasionally. If nothing else, it serves as a reminder that I should give thanks for the way my life has changed since then. (But sometimes I wonder, what if it hadn't changed? What then? Would I have learned by then to give thanks anyway?)

We traveled by very different routes to that destination, you and I, and we are quite different people. I, older than you by at least twenty years, native Minnesotan and lifelong Catholic; you from the South, devoted Christian and wife of a Protestant minister. One of the things that brought us together was our mutual puzzlement that such a terrible thing could happen to people who believe in a loving God, who pray, who have always tried to be faithful. How could we be stricken with such a hellish disease? One of the many torments we suffered that summer was having our faith put to such a test.

You had experienced some dramatic changes in your life that you had to work through and settle. I was dealing with a recurrence of cancer, had finished radiation and begun chemotherapy. I was wearing a body brace, walking with a cane, fighting weakness and pain, and trying to face the reality that this might be my final illness, or at best the beginning of a very limited life. With that in mind, I was assigned time in the occu-

pational therapy kitchen, where I was instructed in ways to prepare meals while using a walker or wheelchair.

The Fourth of July is a memory arouser that comes regularly by the calendar. Others arise by themselves unexpectedly.
Never before or since have I watched the television show "The
World's Funniest Home Videos." Never before or since have I
gone to a stupid "Ernest" movie. But when I see them scheduled
in the paper, I'm back at the Unit again, remembering the shows
we watched in our desperation to pass the time, to get one more
day to go by.

That moronic "Ernest" movie was one we all watched until
very late one night, shoving bedtime off as long as we could, a
nightly effort. We wanted to delay the sleeping pill (and my pain
pill) till the last possible moment, hoping against hope that sleep
would come and last through the entire night. The first topic of
conversation each morning was how much sleep we had managed to get the night before. Fortunate was the person who
could report sleeping all the way through till five or six. We all
knew how devastating it was to wake up, sleep finished for the
night, and discover it was only 2:00 a.m.

Jigsaw puzzles and certain card games are memory joggers
too. I had avoided card playing all my life, could always think
of a dozen things I would rather do. The fact that I actually
played cards that summer indicates how desperate I was. They
were games that even our youngest grandchildren already knew
well—Kings in the Corner, for one. In the closet behind me are
the jigsaw puzzles from that time, another form of recreation
begun in the Unit. These were close at hand the first weeks after
I came home, one always in progress on the card table.
Reminders on all sides.

Sometimes now when I read those Gospel passages where
Jesus drives out an "evil spirit" or "demon," I like to imagine
that some were the demons of depression. No wonder the trans-
formed person went off "praising and thanking God." Who
wouldn't! No wonder they couldn't keep their healing secret, as
Jesus often told them to. Their astonished family and friends
would surely insist on knowing what caused the miraculous
change. I think we all went to bed each night hoping to discover

in the morning that such a transformation had happened for us. But it was a much slower process, inch by inch.

That was the summer I learned what a "split second" is. It was the moment of waking each morning and feeling for one fraction of a second that all was well. It's the shortest mini-second I've ever experienced, for instantly the leaden blackness pushed through and settled in for another day. There it lay, a physical presence.

One of the many things I admired about you, Barbara, was the way you refused to hide out in your room, a temptation we all faced. Of course, we all went to the required therapy and educational sessions, but it took our own initiative to use the games and activities provided. Here is a note from my journal on July 9:

> Barbara left today—I am going to miss her terribly. She has been an inspiration to me—making herself go to all the activities, playing games, working on the puzzles, doing needlework, talking to people. Our natural inclination is to avoid such things, and yet they are the very things we most need for healing. I can sense that other patients also see something special in Barbara. I hope she will thrive and get well at home.

There was an underlying assumption on which our therapy was based: that behind every serious depression lay an unresolved anger turned inward. We were supposed to be able to identify that anger and then write letters to the person or situation that caused it. I don't remember how successful you were with that, but I never could quite figure out who or what I was supposed to be angry with. In the end I simply wrote angry letters to the cancer and then to the depression itself.

We both thought that the group sessions with the chaplains were valuable. It was they who assured us that it was all right even to be angry with God and to express that anger. God knows our innermost thoughts anyway, so we could count on being understood. I agree with that, but I could honestly say that I was not angry with God—at least not over my situation. (Maybe a couple of other things, but not this!) In fact, my overriding emotion was sheer terror, not anger.

I'm sure you recall as well as I do the woman who had no trouble at all knowing where *her* anger came from. She was still filled with rage over the death of her mother twenty years earlier at the hands of a drunk driver. And she *did* blame God. I can still see and hear the way she almost snarled through her tears, "I don't believe in a loving God. A loving God would *never* let this happen to a mother of young children." She grieved for all the conversations she and her mother never had. It was a chilling moment. There was so little help we could offer her.

We surely were a mixed group, weren't we? Old, young, women, men, one religious sister, professional people, teens. We came to care about one another very much, rejoiced with the one who went home, grieved with the one who had a setback, had to change medication, and start all over. A journal entry I made one morning might bring back memories for you too:

> The scene: here in the lounge, the TV is set on a pattern of red, green and blue, and there is country music from a radio station playing on it. Ed [I've changed all the names] is stretched out on one sofa, biting his nails, wearing a white tennis visor and pointy cowboy boots. On another sofa, staring into space is Millie, 88 years old and a die-hard Twins fan. I sit here in my mauve recliner, trying to occupy my time writing. Out in the main area, a new woman, seriously disabled, sits in her wheelchair and stares. Edith, who is still angry and won't speak to me, sits at the table; a young mother just received visitors, her husband and year-old child. A steady stream of smokers comes and goes past my chair into the smoking room.
>
> Gerry, one of our newest additions, paces and paces, back to her room, out to the lounge, sits a few seconds, then gets up and paces some more. I can get her to smile occasionally with a greeting, but most of the time she is completely silent. Dear God, there are some sad stories in here. Have mercy on us all!

Every day our membership changed as new patients came and healing patients went home. We could tell how long people had been there simply by watching them at mealtime. New arrivals sat in silence, staring, picking at their food, weeping. Those who had been there longer talked with one another, maybe even laughed a bit, spoke of plans for their return home—most of their tears had been shed. I wonder where and how they all are today.

Anyone reading this over my shoulder would envision the Unit as a hellish place, all gloom and darkness. It seemed that way at times, I suppose. But it was also a wonderful, nourishing, safe place to be. We were surrounded and supported by women and men who took the time to listen to us, reassure us, help us sort things out, and give us hope. When they sensed that one of us was having a bad moment and needed help, they set aside whatever they were doing to make themselves available.

The medicine we needed most at the beginning was hope; we got generous doses of that from the staff, who kept assuring us that, yes indeed, people do get well. Our hope was boosted when we saw a patient recover and go home. (But how shaken I was when one woman told me she was there for the third time. Such a possibility had never occurred to me.)

You remember Tom, of course, that gentle man who loved music and listened to tapes by the hour. I wrote this about him one day:

> Tom just stopped by my recliner to say good night. He got himself a new harmonica and is teaching himself to play. Now *there* is an instrument I could probably play—even stretched out in a recliner! He will be leaving tomorrow—a big change has come over him during the past two days, and he is ready to face the world again. He will be missed here, such a gentle and thoughtful man.

One of the hardest things of all was that it was impossible to pray. Time after time I sat with my Bible in hand, turning to my favorite psalms, usually a reliable refuge in times of trouble. It didn't work. Every attempt just triggered more tears. (I calculate that I made up for forty years of unshed tears that one summer.) In our sessions with the chaplains we were told not to be distressed about our inability to pray—the days and nights of suffering would be our prayer. So that's what we offered. Most nights I found that all I could do was simply hold my rosary in my hand as I lay in bed.

Did you save the writing assignments we were given as part of our therapy? It was more than two years before I had the courage to look at mine and at the journals I kept that year. It was unbearably painful. Looking through them again today brought back things which I can smile at now but which were anything but amusing then. A supposedly wise person once wrote, "If you are going to be able to laugh at it later, you can laugh at it now." Not necessarily.

For instance, today as I was leafing through those hospital papers, a newspaper clipping fell out, a "Dear Abby" column from that year against open-casket funerals. I have no memory of saving it—or ever seeing it—but there it was. I laughed when I saw it today, but I doubt if it was funny to me the day I clipped and filed it away. What do you suppose I was thinking? I can make a joke now of the relaxation tapes I listened to in the hospital. A slow, soothing voice would say "You are now growing more and more relaxed. You are at peace," and I would shout in my head, "No! I'm not! I'm not relaxed at all!" It strikes me funny now, but it was maddening then.

In his book *Further Along the Road Less Traveled*, M. Scott Peck quotes Donald Nichol, who says, "We cannot lose once we realize that everything that happens to us has been designed to teach us holiness."[2] I hold that thought up against memories of those weeks in the hospital and ask what, if anything, we learned. At the time I saw nothing in it except the blackest kind of suffering. Then you and I began exchanging letters, reporting on our return home, the hills and valleys we experienced as we eased back into life. Ever so gradually, we both noticed something precious emerging.

It happened for me, I suppose, because I was too dumb or naive to keep my mouth shut. I spoke very openly about having suffered a depression and spending two weeks in the mental health unit. People were amazed to hear me say what a healing place I thought it was. I hadn't taken into account what a stigma is still attached to such mental illness. Often after I had spoken out, others came forward cautiously to tell how they, too, had been on medication for depression at one time or had visited a sister or husband in the Unit. I could see they were grateful (as well as shocked) that I had spoken of it openly and without shame. Your letters told of the very same thing happening to you. All the time I was in the hospital, I had hoped and tried to pray that eventually some good would come from that awful time. Now I began to see what it was: it was now possible for us to give others reason to hope.

Never was this more pointed than a recent spring when I was part of a panel at our college homecoming. Each panelist was asked to speak on challenges we had had to face and overcome. My emphasis was to be recovering from breast cancer, and I mentioned the depression as part of that process. During the question-and-answer period, not one woman in this large audience of women asked a question about the cancer, but there were many questions and comments about depression. That's the part of my story they most needed to hear. Your letters told of similar experiences in your world. One of them says it especially well. You wrote:

> I am surprised sometimes at the thoughts I have about the "journey" we shared. Surprised to hear thoughts such as . . . "I am glad (!?) I have experienced this" or "I am helping this friend or this family member with what I went through" or "I can see God's purpose in this time of pain." How can God take pain and make it useful in our lives to the point we say, "Thank you . . . because I wouldn't have known otherwise."
>
> It helps me relate so much better to so many people and that is amazing to me. Now I count it a privilege to have God send someone my way because He trusts me and has entrusted me with this "knowledge."

Such positive thoughts would have been unthinkable in the midst of that dark valley, yet here we were experiencing that very same thing. I began to think of the depression as a resource we had now that we didn't have before, a treasury we could draw from to comfort others. (Though I would prefer it, Lord, if you would please make no further deposits into my account.) Sometimes all that was needed was for someone to see that we had made it back. There was that gift of hope again.

I don't know whether I ever told you that sometime later I asked the psychiatrist what could have triggered my depression. It seemed so out of character for me, I thought. He said the fact that medication brought relief meant that there had been a chemical imbalance of some kind in the brain. But what caused the chemical imbalance, I wanted to know. I was told it could have been the cancer itself, a reaction to treatment or medication, emotional factors, or all these plus others. For me it remains a mystery.

I can now pray the psalms again, though some have a new twist. You are familiar with the psalms that speak of being saved from those going down into the "pit." You can guess what I now think of as that pit. Psalm 116 especially sums up those days for me, and the healing days that followed:

> Return, O my soul, to your tranquillity,
>   for the Lord has been good to you.
> For he has freed my soul from death,
>   my eyes from tears, my feet from stumbling.

By the time summer ended and fall began, that had become literally true for me.

It seems that with each major event in our lives we change the way we pray to incorporate that new experience. It never occurred to me before to pray for people suffering from depression, but I do now, and especially for all who are patients in the Unit right now. I think of them especially on weekends. Remember how endless Saturdays and Sundays seemed, with no classes or activities programmed? And you may be sure that when I hear the Fourth of July fireworks, I breathe a prayer for whoever is seeing that display from the solarium where we once sat.

For some time after that summer, I didn't care much for the Serenity Prayer. That plaque I painted has long since been discarded. I discovered that the familiar lines are actually only the beginning of the prayer; the best part comes in the later lines and would be a good daily prayer for anyone. I have added it to the list of coping skills we learned in the hospital:

> God, grand me serenity to accept the things I cannot change, courage to change the things I can, and wisdom to know the difference; living one day at a time, enjoying one moment at a time; accepting hardship as a pathway to peace; taking, as Jesus did,

this sinful world as it is, not as I would have it; trusting that you will make all things right if I surrender to your will; so that I may be reasonably happy in this life and supremely happy with you forever in the next.

—Reinhold Niebuhr

You would appreciate a homily I heard this very morning. The reading was the story of Joseph in Egypt finally revealing to his brothers that he was the one they had sold into slavery years before. A thoroughly evil, treacherous act had been turned into a blessing. How could anyone have seen at the start that it was all part of God's plan for saving his people? Joseph said, "Even though you meant harm to me, God meant it for good, to achieve his present end. . . ." Our "detour" (your word) was like that; we came to recognize the gift only later.

Once again, Barbara, I thank you for your friendship, your wonderful letters and supporting prayers. I'll end with a cheery quote from Thomas More: "You pray for me, as I will for you, that we may *merrily* meet in heaven!" (I've emphasized the "merrily," antidote to the sad times we shared.)

With love and hope,

Pat

To Patient Griselda of "The Clerk's Tale"

Another Look at Patience

Dear Griselda,

I hadn't given you a thought in many a year until one day recently when the conversation turned to the subject of patience. That's when your name surfaced and I remembered meeting you in a Chaucer class long ago. For five centuries you have been renowned as "Patient Griselda," the main character in a tale told by one of the pilgrims on the way to the shrine at Canterbury. Now I find myself resurrecting your story as I consider that mysterious virtue of patience.

Poor Patient Griselda! Your history reads like the typical fairy story.[1] You were the daughter and only child of a poor man, in fact "the poorest in all the village." In typical fairy-tale fashion, you were the fairest and most virtuous of maidens, even though you came from such miserable surroundings. You were, according to the storyteller, not just beautiful but also "diligent, obedient, reverent, mature and staid in temper, wise." No doubt about it, you were a perfect woman, at least by fourteenth-century standards.

Your life took one of those incredible turns that happen regularly in fairy stories when the richest, kindest, and most virtuous young nobleman (handsome, too, of course) chose you to be his wife. He was Walter, the marquis who ruled that part of the country. His servants took off your ragged clothes and dressed you in gold. "They combed your hair, which lay untressed full rudely, and covered you with gemmed ornaments, great and small." And off you went to a fabulous wedding at the palace.

"And to drive forth this tale quickly," as the storyteller says, you were so gracious and favored in every way that Walter's subjects could hardly believe that you had come from such humble beginnings, for you behaved like a woman descended from a noble line. In fact, you were "so discreet and fair of speech, so benign and so worthy of reverence, and knew so well how to hold fast the people's hearts, that everyone who looked upon your face loved you." The people were delighted when you had your first child, a lovely daughter. Everyone, including you, would have preferred a man-child, we are told, but at least this daughter proved that you were not barren. Thus you could cling to the hope of being blessed with a son later. (You will excuse a hint of twentieth-century irony, I hope.)

For some ungodly reason that we Chaucer students could never understand, your husband, though he loved you dearly and trusted you completely, decided to test you. He began by telling you (and it was a lie) that his subjects were complaining that once your children inherited the crown, the people would find themselves ruled by someone whose mother had been of "poor and lowly estate." Because of their insistence that they didn't want to be in servitude to such a one, he said, the child must die. Your husband sent one of his men to pick up the child, and you were told you would never see her again.

Did you object and argue, rant and rave, weep and plead, rage and scream, hide the child, send for help? No, tearless, you kissed the child goodbye, asking only that the man who took her should bury her body deep enough so the birds and beasts could not get at it!

What you didn't know was that Walter had your little girl taken to a relative in Bologna, who raised her in "all gentle breeding." Not once after that did you ever complain about this strange command, shed a tear, or even refer to it. Always Patient Griselda, you remained serene and uncomplaining. Your husband kept searching for signs that you were angry or grieving, but he could find none. You had apparently passed the test: "No chance sign of any affliction" did you ever show, nor did you ever mention your daughter's name, "in mirth or sadness." By this time we students reading your story were rolling our eyes at each other and having serious doubts about you.

Well, I don't have to tell you the details of what happened next. Four years passed and you gave birth to a son. When the boy was two, your husband again felt the need to test you, though you had already proved yourself time and time again. He did the same dreadful thing he had done before—he sent the child off to Bologna and left you thinking he was dead. Again you begged the servant who took the child to bury him in a place that would not be molested, and went back to behaving as if nothing had happened.

At this turn of events, I know what some of us Chaucer students were thinking what *we* would do in your place. Not you, though, not Patient Griselda. And the worst was yet to come. Years passed, and your daughter matured into a beautiful young woman. Now Walter decided on one more test. He arranged to get some forged letters from the pope, giving him permission to set you aside and marry someone else—for the good of the people, of course. And who was the new bride to be? Your daughter. (As I write this letter, I'm beginning to think this story sounds a lot like those summaries of today's soap operas that I see in the paper.) In vain did your husband look for some sign of emotion on your face; you, a "flower of wifely patience," remained "staid and constant as a wall."

Your husband sent you home in rags while he prepared to welcome the new bride. But then, deciding that you would be the perfect person to arrange things at the castle (after all, who would know better?), he called on you to supervise the preparation of the marriage feast and the sleeping arrangements. Did you refuse? Of course not. You were still the faithful and loving wife. You answered, "Not only, lord, am I glad to do your pleasure now, but in all things I desire also to serve you and please you in my degree without fainting, and shall evermore." You even praised his good choice in marrying such a lovely woman and wished them both "prosperity and pleasure." We students were nearly gagging by now.

Only at the very last minute before the wedding did Walter break down and reveal the whole incredible plot. Finally you showed some real human emotion: you "fell down in a swoon for piteous joy." And this is hard to believe, but you thanked your "benign" husband for not actually killing the children but having them "tenderly guarded." Naturally, all the people rejoiced, and you lived happily ever after.

I can't help wondering, though, if at some time in your old age when you and your husband were alone, you weren't tempted to ask, "Walter, honey, what in the world were you thinking of when you did those terrible things to me?" If I were that daughter sent off to Bologna, I think I would have a few questions of my own. Had you lived in my place and time, Griselda, somewhere along the line you would have been referred to a counselor, signed up for assertiveness training, and begun work on your faulty self-image. As for Walter—well, he would be getting some help in a support group for husbands who are emotionally abusive to their wives.

Seriously, though, the storyteller does draw some interesting morals at the end. He says that the world nowadays is "not so strong" as it used to be, so wives should not try to follow your example of humility—it would be "intolerable." I think we could agree with that. He then comments that in any town today we would be lucky to find three Griseldas, or even two. That's because today's women are not pure gold, as you were, but "alloyed with brass" and would rather break in two than bend. (This "today" he refers to is the fourteenth century. I shudder to think what he would say about us women of the twentieth century. I wonder, too, was he the first man to call women "brassy"?)

The principal moral seems to be that *every* person should be "firm in adversity" as you were. The author adds, "For since a woman was so patient toward a mortal man, much more ought we to receive in meekness all that God sends us; for there is great reason that He should test what He has made."

Well, Griselda, this leads me back to our discussion of patience. Exactly what is it, and what is God expecting of us? Are we really supposed to hold you up as an ideal? I'm discovering that there is much more here than meets the eye. At first glance, patience looked to me like a simple, garden-variety virtue, with none of the nobility of faith, hope, and charity. Taking a closer look, however, I've discovered how varied patience can be, how it changes with our time and circumstances, how very heroic it really is. But I guess I don't have to tell you that.

When I began looking at what people over the centuries have written about patience, including what I found in the Scriptures, I discovered two schools of thought. One group speaks of patience as a tough, strong virtue. One writer even compares "stubborn patience" to "triple steel." Another says that the "strongest of all warriors are these two—Time and Patience." Someone else sees patience as a "necessary ingredient of genius." "Beware the fury of a patient man," warns another.

A gentler view is taken by St. Francis of Assisi. He promises that "where there are patience and humility, there is neither anger nor vexation." Shakespeare, always dependable for a pithy comment, observes, "How poor are they who have not patience / What wound did ever heal but by degrees?"

It is more likely that you would have heard biblical examples of patience. A poor fourteenth-century woman wouldn't have been able to read, I suppose, but I think you might have heard Bible stories and admonitions in Sunday sermons. Maybe you were impressed by what St. Paul says in his letters, for example when he tells the Romans that they should be able to "derive hope from the lessons of patience." (Did you derive any hope, Griselda?) He tells the Ephesians that they should act "with perfect humility, meekness and patience, bearing with one another lovingly." (Exactly the way you behaved toward Walter all those years—had this passage inspired you?)

Maybe what impressed you most was not words but stories of patience in action: Abraham and Sarah waiting all those years for the long-promised son, to the point that Sarah couldn't help but laugh at the very idea; Joseph of Egypt being sold into slavery by his brothers and sorely tested for years before triumphing; Moses and those forty hard years in the desert; St. Paul's long periods in prison even while doing God's own work. Might such dramatic stories of patience have shaped your thinking and behavior?

From my twentieth-century angle, it looks as if patience, though it always requires some kind of waiting, wears a variety of faces, faces that change over time. When I was a young mother and our children were small, patience to me meant not being crabby, remaining cheerful with the children no matter how tired I might be or how loud and messy things got. (I read somewhere during those days that to raise children successfully it helped to have a liking for noise and dirt.) I prayed for patience every morning and confessed failures in it every night. I doubt that you ever had such a problem, Griselda.

As the children grew, patience took on a different look. The waiting then was for a teen to get home with the car, for letters to arrive, for the SAT scores to come, for some bill to be finally paid off. (I phoned our dentist once to call his attention to the fact that our bill had just been paid in full, after years of making a monthly payment as regular as rent. I didn't want him to miss the moment.)

Now that we are older and the children are grown, there is still some unavoidable waiting, but again its face has changed. Sometimes it has meant waiting for a biopsy report, for recovery from surgery to be complete, for tests to show if the treatment has worked. Most of the time now, though, I see patience as a willingness to let events unfold at their own pace instead of trying to force them. I frequently experience this when I am working on a creative project. Now and then I have to walk away from it, let it gestate awhile, and later come back for a fresh look. I find that it unfolds more naturally on its own after such a recess. It works the same with troubled relationships, annoyances, upsetting news, feelings of anger.

You know, Griselda, I think I may owe you an apology. Reading through this letter, I realize now how cynical I have sounded at times. Not that you would ever show any hurt feelings, heaven knows. I couldn't imagine why such an improbable person as you should be held up as an example. Now, however, I believe the key is in that statement I mentioned before, where your storyteller says that "we ought to receive in meekness all that God sends us." I'm thinking now that this story is set before us not to teach what the ideal wife should be in relation to her husband, but what we should all be in relation to God.

Suppose we think of your story as an analogy, with Walter as the symbol for God, and you for the rest of us. Told that way, the tale teaches that no matter what befalls us, good or bad, we should try to accept it without excessive fear or complaint, and even give thanks as you did. Why? Because we trust that eventually the happy ending will come. Unfortunately, that is where our analogy, like all analogies, begins to fall apart. Walter, motivated by that bizarre need to test you, deliberately brought about your sufferings. Worst of all, he robbed you of hope and the comfort of anticipation. You couldn't even ease your pain by looking forward to some happy faraway day when you'd have the children again—to you they were dead.

God is no Walter, thank heaven. I am convinced that God does not deliberately design suffering as a test for us, nor does God desire us to bear injustices of the kind Walter heaped on you. Rather, knowing that we will certainly be tested in this life, God comes to walk our journey with us and help us bear the load. Who knows, perhaps part of that load may involve fighting just such injustices as you experienced. Whatever our path may be, we can be sure that God's plans for us are "peace and not disaster." Gradually we learn that it's safe to "go with the flow." ("Going with God's flow"—could that be another way of defining patience?)

Most important, God holds out hope and the promise of a happy ending. If you had any hope at all, Griselda, it surely didn't come from Walter but from the promises of God.

Just recently I found in a catechism a rather unusual interpretation of patience that made me think of you and the way you handled your tests. I thought you might enjoy hearing it before I end this letter:

> Patience is very close to hope. It means to be on the watch, lovingly but soberly, to note every spark of goodness in the acts of others and every spark of truth in their words. It is without bitterness or rancor.
>
> Patience is one of the loveliest virtues of our times, where so many opinions, grudges and resentments clash and fight it

out. But hope in God should give us the patience not to break off relationships and not to grow hard.[2]

Sounds exactly like you, Griselda. You didn't break off the relationship nor did you grow hard. On one of your saddest days you said to Walter, "Not only, lord, am I glad to do your pleasure now, but in all things I desire to serve you and please you in my degree without fainting, and shall evermore." That sounds like a prayer we could easily adapt for our own use, doesn't it? In fact, it sounds very much like "Thy will be done."

Thank you for helping me with my study of patience, Griselda. You may now go back to your "happy ever after." You deserve it.

With belated appreciation,

Patricia Opatz

To Our Grandchildren

Handing on a Few Personal Treasures

My dear grandchildren,

Some grandmothers create animal cookies or decorate cakes with cartoons. Some take their grandchildren on trips to Disneyland or to the lake to fish. Some give costly presents. Well, you are stuck with a grandmother who likes to write letters—and this one's for you. Dozens of topics come to mind, but I think I will have to settle on just three or four here. You are so wonderfully different from one another, I'm not sure it will work to write one letter to all of you. But I am going to try.

Now that I'm a grandmother, I look back on my life and recognize that certain things have been very helpful to me. (Other grandparents I talk to have similar lists.) These are small things, I suppose, but it turns out that they have enriched my life in enjoyable ways. What I am wondering is whether you enjoy these in your life too. Just in case you might otherwise miss them, I decided to write this letter. Not passing them on to you would be like keeping you from some treasure you have a right to inherit.

The first thing I am wondering is this: Do you know about guardian angels? I don't mean have you just *heard* about them—you must have, there are so many books about angels being published these days. Some of you even have that traditional guardian angel picture in your room. What I mean is, has it made any *difference* to you? Are you aware of the ancient teaching that there is an angel assigned to take a special interest in you? It strikes me that that is quite a wonderful thing to know.

Like all kids these days, you have many things on your mind—situations at school, friendships, growing up, puzzlement about decisions you have to make, your family, the future. Each of you could probably make your own list of things that worry or bother you sometimes. Well, knowing that you have a guardian angel whose assignment is to look after you can be a big help, believe me.

Long ago I decided to give my own guardian angel a name, so I chose the title of a favorite prayer, the *Angelus* (which means "angel"). What a happy surprise it was years later to discover that I have an ancestor by that very name: Angelus Van Hee, a great-great-grandfather on my Belgian side. (Of course, he is now *your* ancestor too.) I felt good about finding that out, as if it meant that I had made the perfect choice.

I talk to Angelus pretty regularly. In fact, I rarely get in the car without asking him to help me drive carefully and protect me. Every day I ask him for some kind of strength or help or clear understanding. The traditional teaching is that angels are creatures of God just as we are, but their role is different. In many cases God has used them as messengers, but also for other special missions. One of those missions is to watch over people like you and me. The Bible tells of many ways angels have assisted those assigned to them. They have appeared to make crucial announcements, keep travelers safe on treacherous journeys, bring people together, free prisoners, warn of danger, fight off enemies, bring enlightenment and guidance. You can see that they are mighty good friends to have.

Your own angel is just such a powerful friend to you, always near and ready to help. It would be a shame if you did not get to know and pray to such an ally. We can ask our angels for help in any situation, as long as what we ask for is a good thing. For instance, you wouldn't expect an angel to help you cheat on a test or rob a bank, but you could certainly ask him (or her) to help you remember everything you had studied.

One other thing. Those pictures that show angels as chubby little babies really bother me. Valentines are some of the worst. They certainly don't look like the angels the Scriptures tell us about. Those angels are powerful, majestic creatures, not sweet little things you could rock on your knee. I can't imagine asking one of those little cuties to give me any protection or guidance in a tough situation.

My Angelus has been a good and reliable friend to me in many ways. I suspect that someday when we meet face to face, I will learn of many times I have been helped out of scrapes that I'm not even aware of now. I wanted you to know this—and encourage you to strike up a conversation and friendship with the angel who is keeping an eye on *you*. You might think about giving your angel a name too. (If you want to see an angel in action, get out your Bible and read the Book of Tobit.)

Though I'm pretty sure you are familiar with angels, I think it less likely that you know much about another comforting truth: the communion of saints. That may sound like a pretty heavy idea, but actually it's a delightful thing to be aware of and to make your life more interesting. It's another way God has of looking after you. Let me tell you about it.

There is a line in the funeral service that says, "For God's faithful people, life is changed, not ended." Death merely moves a person on into another phase of life. Those who have crossed through death into that new life are still close to us. They continue to love us and take an interest in us as much as they did when they were here. Not only that, but we can pray for them, and we can ask them to pray for us. I think the best way to show you what I mean is to tell you a true story.

One of my aunts (who would be your great-aunt) was a longtime grade school teacher. When she died a few years ago, an article written about her said, "As a classroom teacher for thirty-seven years, Sister Marie Louise was exceptionally successful with students who experienced difficulties. Her quiet approach, mixed affectionately with a good sense of humor, sparked a student's willingness to try again and again until progress was made."

Not long after her death one of our grandchildren had to move to a new city and a new school. It was a difficult change, and he was having a hard time of it. Remembering Sister Marie Louise with all her teaching success, her kindness and humor, I began asking her every day to pray for this grandson. I am confident she did, because gradually he began to do better, then to thrive and succeed in ways quite unexpected at first. Just between you and me, I don't think this boy's enthusiasm for music is a coincidence either, for one of Sister Marie Louise's teaching strengths was music. I turned to this great-aunt again when other grandchildren faced a similar change in schools and found it hard to leave favorite activities and close friends. It did not surprise me to learn recently that both are doing well, happy in their new school.

Skeptics say that such happy happenings are mere "coincidence." Don't you believe it. Someone once said, "Coincidence is the language of angels," and someone else, "Coincidence is God's way of remaining anonymous." Your grandmother agrees—there is no such thing as coincidence. I tell you this story as one way to picture the communion of saints. Others in that same communion are all the aunts and uncles, grandparents and great-grandparents you never had a chance to know before they died, as well as all the angels and saints. Don't you find it comforting to know that they are still connected to you in close, caring ways?

You will notice if you have read this far that I talk about prayer as if it were an everyday thing, not something reserved for Sunday mornings in church or in times of crisis. Right! I'm not sure what your experience of praying has been or what you have been taught about it. That's another of those things I wonder about.

Maybe you already talk to God as easily as you talk to your friends. Maybe you already know that you can talk to God about *anything*. I hope so. And if you don't, I encourage you to give it a try. Some people make the mistake of picturing God in a far-off heaven, a distant cloud, but actually it's not like that at all. As one old song says, "God is closer than breathing, nearer than hands and feet." Someone else wrote that God is closer to us than we are to ourselves. You can't get closer than that.

One of the things that makes it easy for us to talk to God is knowing that we can use ordinary, everyday language. We don't have to sprinkle our prayers with "thee" and "thou" and "beseech," but can talk the same way we talk to any other good friend. In fact, with God we can be a lot more outspoken than we dare to be with some friends. Because God already knows what we are thinking anyway, we can be as frank or frustrated or silly or blunt as we like. I love the line from Psalm 139 that says to God, "Even before a word is on my tongue, behold, O Lord, you know the whole of it." So go ahead, feel free to say what is truly on your mind, in your heart.

Many places in the Bible tell us that God "delights" in us. That's something like saying that God gets a charge or a kick out of us, or whatever expression you use these days. I think it's important to know that so we can relax and enjoy God's company. We are much more likely to try to please someone who finds us delightful than someone who scares us to death, don't you think?

Just today as I went through my normal routine, it was easy to keep up a running prayer conversation with God (and sometimes with Angelus). That included an hour at the dentist, driving the car, planning meals, writing letters—all of it. I know that your grandfather does the same thing while working in the garden, painting the house, or taking long drives in the car.

Once we get relaxed and regular about talking with God, we find that *we* also take delight in *God,* not just the other way around. We may discover God's sense of humor and recognize sudden happy surprises as being God's work. (I have a friend who says that popcorn is a sure argument for God's sense of humor—a humorless Creator would never have dreamed up such a funny food.)

The truth is, however, there are times when you just can't find words of your own to say. I find that knowing some prayers by heart is a great help. In my day we had to memorize many prayers, but I'm not so sure you do that today. Perhaps it's considered old-fashioned to commit things to memory today, when you only have to push some electronic button to get all the information you need. But let this old grandmother tell you, those memorized passages are a treasure. They become a carry-along prayer, like a flashlight or extra key that you have handy for emergencies. For me, one- or two-line prayers from the psalms work the best. If it's a sleepless night plaguing you, you can't beat one of my generation's favorite prayers, the rosary, a kind of meditation prayer, soothing and comforting. I suffered one of those sleepless nights recently and decided to pray every prayer

I had ever memorized—passages from the psalms, prayers going way back to grade school assignments, prayers learned recently, prayers for every sick and suffering person I knew, and those I didn't know. I felt very wealthy having that supply of prayers at the ready—good, time-tested ways of talking with God.

Suppose somebody is really bugging you, making your life miserable. Whether it's a classmate, a friend, a teacher, someone in your own family (it happens, doesn't it?), try this: pray for them. No, not that they will be struck by lightning but that good things will happen to them, that they'll get their heart's desire. It can be as simple as saying, "God bless him or her." Change every vengeful thought into a blessing for them. I grant you it sounds weird and it isn't easy. But give it time, and you will be pleasantly surprised by the results. No, it isn't magic—it's mystery. One of the mysterious results of praying for others is that while they are getting blessed, *you* get blessed too. Prayer is just that mysterious and powerful. It changes things.

More and more studies are currently being published giving scientific proof that prayer is indeed powerful. Carefully controlled experiments prove that sick people who are prayed for recover more quickly and enjoy better health than those who are not prayed for. I am glad for such studies, because some modern minds simply will not take things on faith but must see evidence. How reassuring that science backs up what faith has always known.

You can talk to God about anything in your life that bothers you, but try to remember the good things too. Giving thanks can be a forceful way of praying, especially when it is done during the rough times of our lives. It concentrates our attention away from what is negative and helps us appreciate all the good that surrounds us. Do you think it's true, as someone once wrote, that it's impossible to be thankful and sad at the same time?

In most areas of our lives we find that we need reminders. Some people make lists, post notes for themselves, try the old string-on-the-finger or rubber-band-around-the-wrist trick for remembering. It's the same with prayer. The Church has a name for such official reminders as incense and holy water and rosaries: "sacramentals." These not only remind us of God but actually have behind them the prayer of the whole Church. We can also create our own unofficial sacramentals from things that have special meaning for us. You have probably seen one of mine without realizing that you were looking at a "sacramental." I mean the tiny gold baby ring that I wear on a chain around my neck. That ring was a gift to me the day I was born and has been with me ever since, so in a very real way it is a symbol for my entire life. It resembles my life in another way too: a circle has no beginning or end, like life, which goes on forever into eternity. You know how you tend to finger something that hangs around your neck? Well, I often find myself doing that with my little ring. Each time I do, it is a reminder to breathe a quick prayer of thanks to God for my life—all of it, the bad as well as the good. I wonder how many hundreds of times I have done that very thing.

You must have things that would be good reminders for you—a medal, a certain picture or statue, anything really, as long as it speaks to you. What we need to remember is that the world is filled with God; every inch of it, everything in it, speaks of its Creator. As one writer has said, there is a "thinness" about everything in the world that reveals the divine beneath it. That is where our reminders, our sacramentals, come in—they remind us of that "thinness," that presence of God behind all that we see.

One last thing that I wonder about: over the years, many of you have received Bibles or books of Bible stories as gifts for first communions and other special events. Do you read them? I can think of three good reasons why you should.

First, because some of those stories are just plain good stories. We always tried to choose books for you that had vivid, attention-grabbing illustrations, the kind of pictures that let you know this was going to be exciting to read. Think of David and Goliath, Joseph and his brothers, Samson, Moses, Joshua and the walls of Jericho, Daniel in the lions' den. People have actually made movies and Broadway musicals out of some of those stories, that's how good they are.

Second, a college professor told me once that students who were not familiar with Bible stories were at a disadvantage in many classes because they did not understand the frequent biblical references great writers use. Students had no idea what such things as these referred to: the thirty pieces of silver, Joseph's many-colored coat, the belly of the whale, manna in the desert, the patience of Job, the wisdom of Solomon, the good Samaritan, the prodigal son. They were strangers to persons like Lazarus and Mary Magdalene, Ruth and Esther. All these and more are in your Bible.

But the third is the best reason of all: because the Bible contains God's own word, a living word, it will help us to know God personally so that we can become friends. If we are faithful about reading it, a little bit at a time, thoughtfully, it can help us in many ways. It gives us guidelines for life and answers about death. It can ease our fears, comfort us when we are down, assure us of our importance in the eyes of a loving God, teach us to pray. The Bible is no ordinary book—it has power. But only if we read it; it doesn't do a thing for us just sitting on our shelf gathering dust.

So those are a few of the treasures of my life that I wouldn't want you to miss. I hope you will take them up, try them out, and find them as precious as they have been for me. I believe that in the long run you will find them even better than than a trip to Disneyland. Honest!

Much love to you all,

Grandma

To Hallmark Cards

About Opening Gifts

Dear Hallmark Cards:

I have just finished a tour of one of your inviting Gold Crown shops, paying special attention to the huge display of gift wrap. Very impressive! Besides large selections of plain colors, foils, and tissues, you have gift wrap for every imaginable occasion and person. For children, even a partial list would include cowboys and dinosaurs, airplanes and balloons, teddy bears and Bugs Bunny, cows and baby dolls, robots and handprints. For teens, there is another whole collection: discs, dancers, food, graffiti, comics, caps, and confetti—whatever your designers think will appeal to the adolescent. Clearly intended for the males on one's gift list are stripes and plaids, sailboats and golf gear, antique maps and pyramids, sphinxes and (would you believe?) boxer shorts. Designed for women, no doubt, are the peonies and tulips, paisleys and granny squares, quilt patterns and butterflies. There are also specialty papers for every holiday from January through December.

After noting more than fifty patterns, I gave up counting. Yours is the kind of gift wrap one wants to remove carefully without tearing so it can be used again, and nobody would think of discarding one of your beautiful bows. I couldn't help but smile, as I window shopped in your store, letting my mind wander over some events of recent years.

My musings led me to an idea for a new line of gift wrap, and I thought I'd run it by you to get your reaction. Off in a corner somewhere, away from the flowers and sailboats, balloons and pandas, you could have a display of slightly soiled, wrinkled brown paper and tangled wads of string obviously used before. Maybe some twisted sealing tape would fit in too. Ideally, the paper would be stiff and hard to shape around a package, yield no clue as to what is inside, and in general be totally unappealing. Some of the best gifts I have ever received came in wrappings along that line.

It all started with an unusual wedding homily I heard a few years ago. Instead of speaking about the importance of loving, as we frequently hear at weddings, this pastor spoke about the importance of letting ourselves *be* loved, about *accepting* love from others. I recall being struck by the novelty of that idea as a wedding theme and made a mental note to think about it later when I had more time.

Before that time came, several other events occurred until finally I began to get the message. Apparently I hadn't been paying attention. Perhaps you have had similar episodes in your life, when you finally notice how many little hints you have been receiving and think it's time to see what lesson they are trying to teach.

One of those events was a milestone wedding anniversary, for which the children wanted to give us a major party. I hated the idea, dug my heels in to keep it from happening, argued how I hated big gatherings and being the center of attention, was sure it would be imposing on people, and be way too expensive besides. I used every argument I could think of. But the rest of the family insisted and persisted—and the big event came to be. It was wonderful! There was such an outpouring of love and affection and happy memories that I winced to think I might have missed it and kept others from enjoying it too.

Another event was an invitation to the state prison located in our city for a special thank-you dinner for people who had been volunteers over the years. I dreaded going to another big gathering of people I didn't know very well. I tried to think of some way to avoid it gracefully, hoped to send my husband instead, but in the end I had to go. You would have thought I was a prisoner heading there for solitary confinement, not a guest going to dinner. And wouldn't you know, it turned out to be a rich and stimulating meeting. I had a chance to meet and talk with good people and came home aglow with gratitude that I had been there.

After a number of similar incidents, I would find myself on the way home praying, "Well, Lord, it happened again. You had this wonderful present for me, but you had to practically beat me over the head with it before I even recognized it as a gift, much less get excited about opening it."

I remembered that wedding homily and began to see that all those things I had found distasteful or difficult or dreaded were actually acts of love, opportunities. God had offered me some wonderful gifts, and I had been ungracious, to say the least, about accepting them. More than merely ungracious, I had balked, turned my back, complained—and still the gifts came. Slow learner.

I wonder if there are other people (even Hallmark people maybe?) who, like me, miss out on some great gifts because we can't see past the packaging. Usually the thought of "gift" brings to mind the Hallmark kind—a beautifully wrapped package, something to anticipate and accept with delight. With a little remembering, however, we may discover that some of the best gifts God has given us, the most loving and valuable gifts, came in pretty unattractive wrapping—some not even as fancy as plain brown paper. I know that was the case with the anniversary party, the dinner at the prison, and a list I could make that would reach back for years.

I once saw a special tribute on public television for entertainer Bob Fosse, who choreographed and danced in many of the great Broadway and movie musicals of recent times. He said that as a youngster he had had severe physical problems that left him off-balance when he walked. To compensate, he had to adjust the way he moved. Ultimately, he said, it was those adjustments that led to much of his extraordinary style. He commented, "Thank God I wasn't born perfect!" God had given him a gift in a plain brown wrapper, and he was smart enough to accept it and open it up.

Even the Hallmark artists who design such happy papers must recall occasions when an ugly package was unexpectedly delivered to their door. Like me, they might have thought it an aggravation, and only years later realized that it had contained something quite valuable. God is very imaginative about gift wrap, shaping it to fit an infinite variety of situations. One familiar instance is the teacher everyone complains about, like the woman whom students secretly called "Old Cannonball" because she was so strict and insisted on their best work. Years later, however, they brag about having survived her class. She is the one they go back to visit, invite to class reunions, and ask for letters of recommendation.

Two of our sons groaned and complained about their summer jobs at the slaughterhouse: the stench, the backbreaking work, the grisly sights and sounds. Now, however, they delight in recalling their days "in the pit." They boast of what they were able to endure and how it equipped them to face hard assignments later in life.

One of our family legends, a story our children have heard a hundred times, is their dad's account of his awful summer away from home on a farm in North Dakota when he was only seventeen. Desperately homesick, overworked, underpaid, isolated. But they have also heard him tell how that experience prepared him to survive three years away from home during the war without once getting homesick.

Bernie Siegel, well known for his work with the mind-body connection in healing, calls a section of one of his books "Disease as a Gift." He writes, "The worst things in your life have within them the seeds of the best." (Hmm, there might be an inspiration for a gift-wrap design there.) He tells of the time he was surprised and delighted to be told that all he had to do to repair a malfunctioning garbage disposal was to push the "reset" button. Later he said to God, "If you're so smart, why didn't you furnish people with a reset button?" and God answered, "I did, Bernie. The reset button is called pain and suffering."[1] That sounds to me like another way of describing lovely gifts hidden in shabby paper. Siegel makes it very clear, however, that neither he nor anyone else can tell other people that their disease is a gift. Only the recipient can decide that—that is, accept the package and claim what's inside. I have read of many people who did that very thing. They viewed their life-threatening illness (about as ugly a present as you can imagine) as a blessing. Siegel tells of two such patients. The first is a man with brain cancer:

I've learned to live. I love living. I love my family, my friends, my job, everything. And everyone. Every day I wake up and I feel alive! At peace . . . Please excuse the outburst. I get carried away sometimes.

I've been dealing with cancer for more than a year now. I'm almost glad I got it. It's changed my whole outlook on living. I *live* from day to day. I make the most out of every day.[2]

His experience is very similar to that of a woman with breast cancer:

Three years ago, I was graced with cancer. I looked my whole life for a teacher, and it wasn't until I got cancer that I really started to pay attention to the preciousness of each breath, to the momentum of each thought, till I saw this moment is all. All my other teachers gave me ideas. This caused me to directly experience my life. When I got cancer, it was up to me to get born before I died.[3]

The same sense was experienced by a friend at the end of a long slow recovery from pneumonia. She wrote to me: "This illness has been gift to me. I have never felt so deeply possessed by God or so free."

Such unpromising presents come to all of us sooner or later. They can show up at our door as miniature packages, mere annoyances, or they can arrive as big, life-threatening bundles. We puzzle and ponder over the randomness of some trial—why me? why now? It seems a terrible waste to have our lives halted in mid-course, our well-laid plans fouled up. We don't like being forced to evaluate all our assumptions and rethink our future. Only later, sometimes much later, do we discover some unexpected good that has resulted. At the very least, like the people quoted above, we learn not to take things for granted as we once did. Perhaps it has made us better, stronger people, given us a kind of wisdom and compassion we would not otherwise have had. Someone may tell us long afterward that the way we faced our trial helped them though theirs. It's important for us to take note of these experiences so that recalling them later will give us hope when other unappealing packages arrive.

Accepting presents in ugly wrapping takes a special kind of vision. It requires faith in action (what someone called "faithing") to see past the outer layer to the treasure inside. You'd think it would be easy for Christians. After all, our faith is founded on the truth of death followed by resurrection, of Easter surprise after Good Friday. But it's never easy. I think it must be rare for a person to see the suffering as gift while still in the middle of it. Not until long afterward are most of us able to see what good came out of the bad. We might think of these as "Do Not Open Until Christmas" presents—only after a wait do we get to see what good the package holds.

The next time an ugly package arrives at my door, I'll try not to judge it too quickly by its initial appearance. No matter how calamitous it looks, I'd like to keep an open mind and give it enough time to work itself out. Recalling that God's plans for us "are peace and not disaster," I hope I have the patience to wait and trust. I'll remind myself how long it took to discover the treasure hidden in other unsightly packages.

I'll also remind myself of that wedding homily, which is making more sense to me now. I can see that receiving is an essential part of the process of giving. It sets up a kind of circular motion, a loving circle, the opposite of a vicious circle. God blesses us with gifts, we recognize them as gifts and bless God with thanks, God blesses us for our thanks, and we give thanks again. The blessings continue to flow, to us and out from us. But first we have to get past the wrapping and recognize the gift.

Well, Hallmark, this has turned out to be one of those letters we write but never send, the therapeutic kind we write to ourselves in order to work out our feelings or clarify our thoughts. Its message is really for me, not you. But thanks anyway for the prompting I got from visiting your shop.

I am going to adopt and adapt your slogan and remind myself regularly that though it may not be clear at first, God always "cares enough to send the very best."

Thanks for the gentle reminder,

Patricia Opatz

To Miss Manners of Newspaper Fame

On the How and Why of Polite Behavior

Dear Miss Manners,

Twice in recent years I have received your books as gifts: the first, *Miss Manners' Guide to Excruciatingly Correct Behavior,* and later *Miss Manners' Guide to the Turn-of-the-Millennium.* I'm not sure what the implications are when a friend gives me two large volumes (over fourteen hundred pages altogether) dealing exclusively with manners and correct behavior. Whatever her reasons, I have chosen not to take offense, because reading your books is so much fun. It's risky, though. The reviewers are right when they characterize you as "opinionated and astringent," "formidable," "arch," "fierce," "bossy," "ruthless," and "an iconoclast."

It's the same with your newspaper column. Sometimes I marvel that people find the courage to write to you at all, knowing full well that they are exposing themselves to your acid wit. Evidently they consider it worth taking the risk just for the pleasure of receiving one of your prickly responses. As one book review (quoted on your cover) said of you, "In the whole of the literature on [manners] you are not likely to find any wiser or funnier advice . . . . Behind an arch façade of wisecracks and putdowns is a solid and thoughtful commentary on what ails our society." It's true—you have a crisp answer for everyone on every topic.

The range of your expertise is amazing. Checking the table of contents in the *Excruciating* volume, I find the heading "Basic Civilization," under which you include such topics as Common Courtesy for All Ages; Saying No: Silence as a Social Skill; Table

Manners; Conversing; and Unpleasant Facts of Life (which has subtitles ranging from Messy Emotions to Disgusting Habits).

You have provided the Gentle Reader (your way of addressing all who write to you for advice) with sections on Rites of Passage, Marriage, Work, Intermediate Civilization (which includes Types of Parties, Some Stunning and Others Ghastly; plus a helpful section on Social Correspondence); all the way through Advanced Civilization right up to and including Death.

It seems to me that many of the answers you give your readers could be classified as spiritual works of mercy, namely, counseling the doubtful and instructing the ignorant. I am in awe of the way you teach some basic lessons in a few simple words (but always including your little barb). Classic examples are these exchanges:

DEAR MISS MANNERS:

Can you tell me a tactful way of letting a friend know that she is getting too fat?

GENTLE READER:

Can you tell Miss Manners a tactful reason for wanting to do so?

* * *

DEAR MISS MANNERS:

When is a written thank-you note for a wedding gift not necessary?

GENTLE READER:

When no wedding present has been received.

* * *

DEAR MISS MANNERS:

Don't you think that nowadays, in modern life, the old-fashioned custom of the condolence call is out of date?

GENTLE READER:

Why is that? Is it because people don't die anymore, or is it because the bereaved no longer need the comfort of their friends? Miss Manners is always interested in hearing about how life has been improved by modern thinking.

Your talents are called for on many a strange subject, and unfailingly you rise to the occasion:

DEAR MISS MANNERS:
    What do you think of cracking knuckles in public? Do you think it's unladylike or annoying? Please reply immediately, because it is a big issue in my house.

GENTLE READER:
    Cracking knuckles is unladylike, ungentlemanlike, unchildlike, and unpleasant. Please insist that everyone stop it this very minute.

* * *

DEAR MISS MANNERS:
    When is a vase a VAHZ?

GENTLE READER:
    When it is filled with DAH-ZIES.

Thus do you teach short, pungent lessons about being thoughtful of others and not putting on airs. Many of your replies are not so terse but go on for several paragraphs, even whole pages. You provide common-sense rules for every life contingency from womb to tomb. Even those people who think they know all about good manners and have no questions to ask will find your answers enjoyable and informative.

It so happened that over a recent span of days I was reading one of your books at the same time I was reading Matthew's Gospel. It was fascinating to see how many times you and Jesus deal with similar issues of human behavior. You state forcefully in several places that your business is not morals but manners. "Manners," you write, "involve the appearance of things, rather than the total reality." Jesus, of course, deals with the total reality. Whereas you tell us the correct and courteous things to do and say, Jesus gives us the *reason*: we treat others courteously because we are to love one another.

Both you and Jesus teach the importance of giving thanks, for example. In fact, there are twenty references in one of your books just to the importance of writing thank-you notes. And we all know how disappointed Jesus was when only one of the ten healed lepers came back to say thanks to him.

Jesus says, "Offer no resistance to injury." You say, "As for the rudeness of others, Miss Manners finds that is conquered by politeness." You refuse to let other people's rudeness provoke a put-down from you, no matter "how one longs to strike back."

Both you and Jesus also have something to say about the risks of pointing out others' faults. Jesus puts it this way: "Why look at the speck in your brother's eye when you miss the plank in your own?" That sounds a lot like your statement that "it is a law of nature that he who corrects others will soon do something perfectly awful himself."

You spend eighty pages on the correct behavior surrounding weddings, all the way from the engagement through getting along with the new in-laws. Jesus, on the other hand, briefly teaches us the profound *meaning* of the marriage commitment, then at a wedding in Cana thoughtfully prevents embarrassment to the wedding families.

You and Jesus take different approaches to some other sticky aspects of human behavior: hypocrisy, judging others, abusive or bigoted language, ostentation, ambition. Your message is about polite behavior, that is, the appearance of things. Jesus goes deeper; he gets behind the appearances to his rule about love. (I suppose that is the reason he usually omits the barbs that you enjoy so much.)

There is one social area where you and Jesus differ sharply. I refer to what is listed in your table of contents as The Dinner Party, and specifically The Guest List. You propose an elaborate system of ranking potential dinner guests, putting them on lists labeled A, B, or C. On the A list are people you refer to as "sparklies," the dazzling people who can make any party a success. The B list, "like the ideal middle class, should consist of solid citizens with a strong sense of duty." They are expected to listen to the "sparklies" and carry on a reasonably good conversation. Then you have your C list, which, "like poverty, one is always trying to eliminate but can't." I don't even want to speculate who the poor souls in that category might be.

When your lists of possible guests are complete, you cross-file them "by occupation and level of achievement." In your plan, the perfect dinner party would have two "sparklies" from different fields, "four solid listeners and contributors from assorted professions, one charity case, and one mystery guest whose classification will not be clear until after being auditioned at this dinner." Naturally, it is vital that these guests be seated in the proper places—not two "sparklies" together, for example.

For good reason, one keeps these lists in a secret book under lock and key. If things are done right, guests will never find out which list they are on, because the mix will have been such a great success.

What I am wondering, Miss Manners, is what your comment might be on Jesus of Nazareth as a host. Like you, he lays out a plan for the ideal dinner party. His is much less elaborate than yours, you will notice, especially his instructions for the guest list: "Whenever you give a lunch or dinner, do not invite your friends or brothers or relatives or wealthy neighbors. They might invite you in return and thus repay you. No, when you have a reception, invite beggars, the lame and the blind. You should be pleased that they cannot repay you, for you will be paid in the resurrection of the just."

Evidently Jesus followed his own plan (as I'm sure you follow yours, Miss Manners), for we are told that he frequently shared meals with the outcasts of society, the tax-collectors and sinners. He never once mentions any "sparklies," but I suppose even a tax-collector or prostitute could sparkle if the occasion presented itself. Such folks must have been fairly good company, I think, because Jesus dined with them often.

What a scene that must have been! Sometimes I close my eyes and try to picture what one of those gatherings must have looked like—Jesus reclining at table with this unlikely mix of guests. On one side I see a tax-collector, well groomed and richly dressed. Next to him is a beggar complete with rags, crutches, and a sour smell. Moving around the table, I see a first-century bag lady, a poor homeless family, assorted social rejects down on their luck, a woman of questionable reputation pulling her veil close, a few ex-prisoners recently out of jail. The chosen Twelve may also have been there, trying to get used to such unorthodox social events. (The majority of these folks would be lucky to make even your C list.)

What do you suppose they talked about? Wouldn't you love to have joined in and listened just once? Who knows, there might even have been some surprise "sparklies" there, people who never before had been honored with an opportunity to say what they thought or ask questions they'd carried in their hearts for years. It must have been a real coming-out party for some.

A gathering like this was such a scandalous breach of the rules that it's no wonder letter-of-the-law folks were enraged. There may have been no book of etiquette then, but there were definite regulations about everything. As you very likely know, Miss Manners, in Jesus' culture it was forbidden for a Jew to mingle with known sinners. Imagine what an impact this must have made, then, when people saw Jesus eating with these "scum of the earth," treating them like friends for all the world to see.

You who are so careful to treat others with respect and courtesy can appreciate what an experience this must have been for Jesus' unlikely guests. For that little while at least, they were accepted like equals and could forget their daily humiliation and shame. How they must have enjoyed the luxury of feeling good about themselves for a change! Even more telling is the fact that people then reclined while eating, so there was probably a good deal of close physical contact. That Jesus, a holy man and prophet, did not avoid this contact must have made these outcasts feel very clean and accepted.

I have no idea, Miss Manners, what your specific response would be to the matter of Jesus' guest-list philosophy compared with yours. Knowing how unfailingly proper you are in other matters of social behavior, however, I feel confident that you would find much in Jesus' plan to admire. For one thing, at his meals there were always more good things on the menu than food: healing, forgiveness, reconciliation, new life, peace, acceptance, instruction. I trust that this Gentle Reader is not being presumptuous in believing that Miss Manners would have nothing but kind words for such lavish hospitality. I hope you would even agree with the thought expressed in Hilaire Belloc's little verse "Courtesy":

> Of courtesy, it is much less
> Than courage of heart or holiness,
> Yet in my walks it seems to me
> That the grace of God is in courtesy.

A faithful reader,

Patricia Opatz

To Mrs. Beatrice O'Meara

In Praise of Choirs

Dear Mrs. O'Meara,

How strange that I should be thinking of you and writing you a letter after so many years—decades, actually. What prompted me was a remark I overheard from someone behind me as I walked out of church after a recent funeral. It was a pretty unkind comment about the choir, and I have to admit the singing had been rather ragged. I was tempted to turn and lecture this music critic about the virtues of volunteer choirs, even flawed ones, but I managed to keep my mouth shut. That passing remark started me reminiscing about our days in the St. Francis Xavier choir in Windom in the 1940s and about you as organist.

I wish that I had known you better, that we could sit at the kitchen table with a cup of coffee comparing choir stories. But I was only a girl, in junior and then senior high, and you were a grown woman with a husband and children. Although you seemed old to me then, I suspect you were actually younger than I am now. There were several things I do recall about you, however, that color my image of you. One was that, so the story went, you and your husband went to an orphanage and adopted the sickliest, most forlorn looking boy and girl you could find (both of whom you reared to be beautiful people). Another time, when our family was in the process of moving, though we were not especially close friends, you invited us all over for supper. The only detail I recall from that meal is that you set the food and the stack of plates in front of your husband, who filled each plate himself and then passed them till all of us had been served. I thought that was very classy! Unforgettable, too, is your reddish hair, heaped into a bun, but always losing wisps around the neck and ears. I'm not sure, but I think you might have been what today we would call "laid back," an indispensable asset for a church organist.

If we could sit and visit over a cup of coffee, I would ask you to tell me more about what it was like to be a choir member, organist, and director by default in those days. My memories are so vague—too involved with my own life at school, I suppose. Now I realize that at that time, except for the servers, we choir members were the only lay people who played an active role in the Mass.

For all I know, you may have been singing in the heavenly choir for many years by now, but I still picture you pumping away at that old organ in the church balcony. We were a mixed lot: volunteers and draftees of all ages and degrees of talent, several of us still in school, along with some of our parents, an attorney, the barber and his wife, and the Schreibers, including Helen, the other organist, as different from you as she could be. Helen was neat and trim, as I recall, and played with reserve and precision. I remember you as being, well, looser. Just how you divided up the duties, I'm not sure, but it was a major commitment, as church choirs still are. I hope other parishioners were not as tardy as I have been in appreciating the way you both shared your gifts with us.

As I recall, there were at least ten Protestant churches in that town of three thousand, and we Catholics were a small minority. That might have been our excuse for not being a better choir than we were—so few singers to choose from. But the truth is that there were *many* good singers in the parish; they simply would not join up. I read a story recently about an organist who threw empty cough-drop boxes down from the balcony at people who should have been upstairs singing but didn't come. Were you ever tempted to try that? I was. Some of those good singers were in my own family.

Although all my mother and brothers could sing very well (in fact, the boys sang in chorus and small groups at school),

Dad and I were the only ones in our family who joined with you every Sunday as faithful choir members. I think the others just didn't have the courage required for such duty. Instead, they sometimes played the role of critic, safely sitting in the pews below while we labored in the balcony. That at least was a plus: we were hidden away in the balcony, not right out in front as choirs often are now, though we did have to emerge at communion time. Another plus was that this was long before television and recordings had spoiled people for anything less perfect than the Mormon Tabernacle Choir and E. Power Biggs.

Post-Sunday Mass conversations still stick in my mind, perhaps because I heard them more than once. Mother would say something like, "For goodness sakes, Lou, you people were dragging so this morning, I half expected to see a dead body come falling out of the balcony." Invariably Dad's response was that if she thought she could improve matters, she should join us. But she never did. It takes a certain amount of humility to sing in a choir, even more in those days than it does now, because there was no congregational singing to dilute the choir's tremulous efforts. You see, Mrs. O'Meara, *everybody* sings now—or at least they are invited to, and it's all in *English!* Wouldn't that have simplified your life? Because we moved away from Windom so many years ago, I have no idea whether you lived to see the changes that flowed from the Second Vatican Council, encouraging the people to sing and actively take part in everything.

In spite of the difficulties, we had some mighty good moments, though, didn't we? I especially remember the vigor we put into "Resurrexit sicut dixit" at Easter, repeating it like a drumbeat. And some of the songs we did every Sunday at communion time we did smoothly, with feeling: "O Lord, I Am Not Worthy" and "O Sacrament Most Holy" come to mind. We also knew the hymns for Benediction very well, because that was a regular devotion then. The Christmas season found us at our best, though I don't think the people sang along even with the carols. I guess it was when we were challenged with something new that we had our problems. With not a single Latin student among us, there must have been some very creative pronunciations of those ancient prayers before the change to English.

As I mentioned, Mrs. O'Meara, it was the comments heard at a funeral that prompted this letter, yet my memories of funerals during those days are pretty vague, perhaps because we younger members were in school and not able to attend. I'm wondering how you managed then—whom did you get to sing? Was there much talk from the pulpit then about "sharing one's gifts," or "time and talent" forms to fill out?

These days this challenge of finding singers for funerals comes up in every parish. Regular choir members, busy at their jobs, are not available for the unexpected weekday funeral, so volunteers are asked for. My first experience with such a funeral choir came when I was married and had a large family. During the summer, when the sisters couldn't round up enough children to sing for funerals as they did during the school year, some of us mothers volunteered. We recruited until we had a good calling list of women who came faithfully and found it immensely rewarding.

Even then it took humility though. Especially painful was the time the pastor was thanking all the people who had contributed in any way to the funeral—the family, assisting priests, the servers, the cooks, and finally the choir. But he referred to us as "a nucleus of a core of a little choir," making us so small we practically disappeared. That is, I believe, what is known as "damning with faint praise." It happened again when a visiting friend said after a funeral that we had "a nice little choir." I saw them as a darned good choir, people who would set aside their own projects and with only one day's notice come ready to sing. We used to say, only half jokingly, "We may not be good, but we're faithful." Some days we were both.

I have been at funerals where there were some warbly, aged sopranos, rambling basses, and tenors who have never been advised that louder is not necessarily better for those high notes. There might have been a time when I was the one making the snide comment about the quality of their singing, but no longer, not now that I have been there myself. If I hear one caustic word, I have my lecture ready—witness for the defense! More and more the practice has spread of having a special choir of volunteers for funerals, and more and more they are getting to be very good. It's a pleasure to be singing now with just such a group.

How I wish you could join the funeral singers I belong to now, Mrs. O'Meara. Like our choir in Windom, we are a mix of volunteers of varying gifts. Among us are a few regular choir members with excellent voices, training, and experience. But there are quite a few of us amateurs too. (That's a good word, "amateur," from the Latin root *amare,* "to love." Amateur choir members sing because of love.) Unlike the choir in Windom, we are not in the balcony, though we are fairly well sequestered, and we have a superb organ with equally superb musicians to play it. (Just as "charity covers a multitude of sins," their playing covers a multitude of our weaknesses.) It would warm my heart to see you sit before this wondrous organ and play some of our old favorites, a reward for all those years of laboring on that little foot-pumper in Windom. I hope that is one of the heavenly treats you are enjoying now.

One of the challenging things about belonging to a "pick up" choir (like a "pick up" ball team) is that we never really know who is going to show up. Depending on people's schedules, we may have four singers or we may have fifteen. With the whole congregation singing along as they do now, however, even a mere "nucleus of a core" is enough to get the people to join in. We have some wonderful bell-ringing, too, which makes one of the final funeral hymns very moving: "May the angels lead you into paradise. . . ." So things have come a long way in the right direction.

You can tell that I admire the faithfulness of people like you who belong to choirs, especially funeral choirs, and even more especially those who belong to choirs that have their, shall we say, weak spots. I know that liturgical purists cringe when the music is not perfect, notes fall a little flat, one voice hangs over the end when the others have stopped, when the *r*'s come out long and hard (as in "when I in solemn wonderrrrrr"), and I suppose I cringe a little myself. People who criticize act as if the singers don't *know* that they aren't perfect, but we do, and even so we come to sing. I guess our motto could be what one wise person observed about a different issue: "Anything worth doing is worth doing poorly."

Reminiscing with you has kindled a feeling of nostalgic affection for that good group of people who were willing to offer their gifts. Too often, I find, we think of gifted people as those with extraordinary talents—the artist, the soloist, the brilliant speaker. People say, "Oh, he or she is so gifted, but I just don't have any gifts at all." It's hard to get them to realize that all God's children are gifted, that gifts come in a variety of packages and sizes, and sometimes the small ones are the most necessary and useful.

Emma comes to mind. At Holy Angels parish, no matter what question arose, whether it was how to run the coffeemaker, how many potatoes to order for a dinner, what to do about flowers, where certain decorations were put away, what we did last year or the year before about Good Friday, how much money to spend for gifts, or who had the key, it was always "Ask Emma." And Emma always knew. She was gifted. I suspect, Mrs. O'Meara, that you were a musical Emma at St. Francis Xavier all those years ago.

Writing this letter has stirred up a lot of happy memories as well as gratitude for those hours spent around the organ in the balcony. We can never know for certain what early events have influenced the rest of our lives, I suppose, but I'm sure that our shared experience as choir members has made a difference in mine. Thanks for making your musical gifts available and for encouraging mine.

Until we meet again, love,

Pat Gits (Opatz)

P.S. (Later) With the help of an alumnae office and the telephone company, I have just traced your daughter's whereabouts and visited with her on the phone. She told me that you died in 1970 at the age of ninety, so you did live to see Vatican II. She also told me that you always referred to that group at St. Francis Xavier as "The Village Choir," and it was important to you. To answer my question about who sang for funerals, I suspect now it was just you singing soprano, with Mrs. Koziolek taking the alto part. It was wonderful to hear that at one time you had played on the big pipe organ in the St. Paul Cathedral. I'm afraid I really didn't appreciate you at the time, and I'm glad to make up for that with this letter.

To the Samaritan Woman of John's Gospel

The Mystery of the Woman at the Well

Dear Woman at the Well,

I hope you will not be offended by such an impersonal greeting, but I don't know any other name to call you. When we are introduced to you in John's Gospel, you are called simply "a Samaritan woman." That's one of many reasons I think of your story as "The Mystery of the Woman at the Well." I suspect that every person's life holds the same kind of mystery that filled yours. Unfortunately, not all of us are as alert to it as you were. That's exactly what has prompted my letter—the mystery in your life and how you were able to open yourself up to it.

Not knowing your name is only the first part of the mystery. No doubt women from Samaria had names similar to those of other women we meet in Scripture, so you might have been Rachel, Esther, Leah, maybe Martha or Sarah—we simply don't know. In one sense that isn't surprising, for women of your day had no legal standing or official identity. You had to "belong" to a father, husband, brother, or master. In another way, though, it *is* puzzling to me that you remain anonymous. After all, your conversation with Jesus at the well is one of the longest recorded in the Gospels, certainly the longest with a woman. There must have been something very special about you, yet you remain nameless.

That Jesus would speak to you at all is mysterious enough, but that he would actually initiate the conversation is even more surprising. You, and later the returning disciples, are amazed to see it. Jewish men were not supposed to speak to *any* woman in public and were to shun all Samaritans. Even worse, because you Samaritan women were deemed ritually unclean, Jews were not to drink from any vessel you had handled. Yet Jesus breaks all those taboos when he asks you for a drink of water. Why? What does he see in you? How does that make you feel?

The mystery deepens when we see your reaction to his request. A typical woman of your time would probably have kept her astonishment to herself, quietly given Jesus the water he asked for (eyes averted and head bowed, no doubt), and then slipped away to finish her chores. But not you. You want to know how he, a Jew, could speak to you, a Samaritan woman. Not only that, you later actually challenge him to explain himself and the mysterious water he speaks of. You dare to ask questions and you don't back down.

You know for sure that there is something mysterious about this stranger when he starts telling you very personal things about your life. Thus we hear that you have had five "husbands" and are now with a sixth. That detail is all we learn about the externals of your life, but it suggests much more. It makes me think that you must have been very beautiful or very charming or both. One thing for sure, you weren't the shy, subservient person that women of your day were expected to be. Maybe you were one of the town characters, the Elizabeth Taylor of Shechem, the topic of much gossip. It's lucky for us that you *were* on the bold side. If you had been a shrinking violet, there would have been no such memorable meeting at the well, nothing of note to record. It's precisely because you were *you,* weaknesses and all, that we still read about that meeting centuries later and meditate on the meaning of it all.

It's so typical of Jesus that instead of visiting with the most honored and virtuous woman of your village, he picks you—and even uses you for some important work. In fact (amazing fact!), you become an apostle for Christ. Yes, really—never mind the ritual uncleanness and questionable lifestyle—you become an apostle. The word "apostle" means "one who is sent," and Jesus explicitly sends you back to Shechem. On the surface it appears that you are going to call that sixth non-husband of yours, but I suspect that Jesus knows you will tell the whole town. (I notice

that when you head back to town, you leave your water jug at
the well. You have every intention of returning to talk again
with this intriguing stranger.) If it weren't for you and your
boldness with this visitor, your townsfolk would have missed
their chance to hear his good news. How ironic that although
you are an effective apostle and still honored in the Gospel, we
don't even know your name.

There is another sense in which you could be considered
an apostle, I think, or at least a disciple. In several places in the
Gospels, Jesus is asked why he speaks to the people only in parables. His answer is that they are not ready, not yet capable of
understanding the full truth. Only to his inner circle does he explain and clarify. We notice that when Jesus talks to you, however, he doesn't hide his message in parables. Apparently he
considers you capable of hearing the truth straight, a great compliment. It is especially notable that when you bring up the
Messiah, he gives a direct answer: "I who speak to you am he."
Rarely is he so outspoken.

A passerby observing this incident would think it was
merely another accidental meeting like many at the well. But it's
no accident. Here we come to the part of the mystery that intrigues me the most—not so much the incident at the well itself,
but what had occurred before that, inside, in your mind and
heart. You are obviously "shining for the harvest" when you
meet Jesus. Even in that embarrassing moment when he con-
fronts you with your lifestyle, you do not back away. You keep
the conversation going, eager for more. Something has been
happening within your spirit to prepare you for this moment.
You are ready to hear, open to receive.

There are so many questions I would like to ask you about
that. What had you experienced that made you so ready? Did
you pray often? Were you moved by something you heard in
the Scriptures? Were there times when you felt little nudges during the day, some touch of the Spirit that made you stop and listen? Were there nights when you lay awake and prayed or
pondered the meaning of your life? Did you feel a hunger for
God and the things of the spirit, and wonder where you might
find answers? Were you disheartened by your lifestyle and did

you wish you could go back and start all over again? Whatever the route may have been that brought you to this moment, Jesus recognizes that you are thirsty for more than merely water from the well. You are ready for the "living water" of the Spirit.

Most mystery stories have the loose ends neatly tied up at the end. All the questions are answered, the evidence laid out, the solution explained, and the characters all accounted for. Not so with your story. All we know is that after meeting Jesus, the townspeople beg him to stay on in Shechem—and he does, for two whole days. It's frustrating to know absolutely nothing about those two days, not a word about what happened or what was said. I would especially like to know what your role was and whether your life changed after that. Did Jesus help you get your marriage straightened out? Or did you leave it all and follow him? As time passed, did the people change their attitude toward you? It must have rankled the finger-pointers to admit that a scandalous woman like you was the one who had led them to Jesus. I notice that when it was all over, some were still reluctant to give you any credit, but said, "No longer does our faith depend on you. We have heard for ourselves. . . ." Well, no matter what those Samaritans may have thought, I write to tell you how grateful I am for your story, mystery and all.

And it is a mystery all right. If someone had been sent on ahead to find a co-worker for Jesus in Shechem, somebody to help him evangelize when he arrived, do you think your name would have been on the list of prospects? Not likely. Yet Jesus chose you, and through you he changed your whole village. That says something powerful about how God's mysterious ways differ from ours.

I like to remember how that memorable day began for you—exactly like every other day. Nothing special, just the usual routine of getting the water and doing your chores. You had no inkling that by noon it was going to turn into a life-changing day. I wonder if all our lives are like that, holding the same potential for mystery, for fresh starts. When those unavoidable hard times come, when we seem to be getting nowhere, can't pray, see no signs of growth—that's when it will be comforting to think of you at the well. For all we know, there may be silent, mysterious workings of grace going on deep within us at that very moment, as there were for you. In ways we could never suspect, God may be even now preparing us for a watershed moment like yours. Remembering you and Jesus at the well gives me hope that I might be as ready for such a moment as you were.

Writing this letter to you has given me the feeling that I too have met you at the well and we've become acquainted. From now on, you will be a reminder for me of the mystery that surrounds us all the time. I will try to stay alert to those mysterious messages hidden in even the most unpromising moments.

Who knows, perhaps someday you and I will meet and talk at some heavenly well of "living water," and finally then you can tell me your name.

A distant admirer,

Patricia Opatz

To Sister Enid Smith, O.S.B.

Little Things Mean a Lot

Dear Sister Enid,

I promise you, this is the last time I will bring up the subject, but that little incident we shared years ago has been such a happy influence in my life that I really must refer to it just one more time.

As you may recall, it was when I was a student at St. Benedict's and you were the brand new dean of residence. My roommates and I approached you in your office for permission to attend a concert at St. John's—in the *middle* of the week, a bold request in those days. We would, of course, wear our hats and gloves so as not to shame the college or irk the abbot, but could we please go, even though it was Wednesday?

There was a long silence, a *very* long silence, as you looked us over and gathered your thoughts. Then you said those memorable words: "The multiplicity of events on the horizon is staggering." That's all. I think we were left speechless and quickly withdrew to see if we could figure out exactly what you had said. It was certainly not the way most people say no.

For years after that you were embarrassed and apologetic about that incident, for turning us down the way you did. More than once you explained that you were fresh out of graduate school (your Ph.D. in philosophy, I think), unfamiliar with the nitty-gritty of student life, and would do things very differently now.

Well, I am glad it worked out exactly the way it did. I wouldn't have missed that wonderful sentence of yours for anything. Truly it has become part of my personal lore, one of those expressions I use for very special occasions, far better than any I could compose myself.

You were always a model of precision with words. I used to say that students in your philosophy class could take notes as you lectured and end up with a perfect, logical outline. To this day, whenever the story of Moses and the burning bush comes up in the liturgical readings, I think of you. You explained God's "I Am" so clearly that I've never forgotten it. "God's essence is existence," you taught us. That was a major lesson.

But you taught small lessons too. I recall the day you asked for the name of a flower for some sentence you were putting together as an example. I was being a smart aleck, I suppose, because instead of saying the usual "rose" or "tulip," I suggested "anemone"—only I mispronounced it "a-nen-o-me." Registering no reaction at all, you went ahead and used the word in the sentence, pronouncing it exactly right. Since I recall it all these years later, I think you could say I got the point.

Recently another "word" memory came to me. This one occurred some years later, when I returned to St. Benedict's for homecoming. In a conversation with several of us, you said that you had grown "curiouser and curiouser" about something. How odd, I thought, that someone as brilliant as you would use that strange word instead of the correct form, "more and more curious." Only later did I realize you were quoting Alice from *Through the Looking Glass*. You were paying me the compliment of assuming I would recognize that famous phrase from a classic story, but I didn't—not then.

That original incident in your office was a very small thing, infinitesimal really. It was just one of hundreds of exchanges that took place during my years at St. Benedict's, most of which I don't remember. Yet here I am, decades later, recalling your exact words from that brief conversation. Besides showing what power words can have, I think my remembering it suggests that the seemingly trivial things in our lives can actually be very important. Little did I realize that day how many times your words would come to mind over the years and fit other wholly unrelated situations. That's what prompted this letter. I thought you might like to know about the ways in which your "multiplicity of events" has surfaced again and again.

I hope you won't mind that I tampered with your words a bit. I did with them what I frequently do with the psalms when I want one to fit a particular occasion: I change or add a word. Your statement became even more versatile and useful to me when I added "small." (In fact, I once decided that if I ever wrote my autobiography, I would call it *A Multiplicity of Small Events,* a fairly good description of most people's lives, I suppose.)

I think of your words each Christmas when we see replays of the movie *It's a Wonderful Life.* The hero, on the verge of suicide, is given a chance to see how different the world would be if he had never lived. He is amazed to discover how many lives his own life has touched and changed for the better. For years it had been happening in ways he had never been aware of or could even have imagined. His life had counted, even when to him it seemed to be a failure. He had been where he was supposed to be and done the multiplicity of small things he was called to do. Truly, it was "staggering" for him to see how important those little things had been.

Your words came back to me again some years ago when I read about a program at a gerontology center in which older people were invited to write their life stories. Some refused, others were hesitant. "Oh, my life was very ordinary," they would say. "There's really nothing to tell." The whole idea sounded too grand and very intimidating. Once they were assured that they would be writing only a little at a time and wouldn't have to show their writing to anyone else unless they wished, they began. Each week they would write a chapter, two pages long, on some specific area of their lives. The following week they would gather in small groups to discuss what they had remembered and written. The subject for the week might be the first house they lived in, childhood Christmases, their first job, their first love, school days they recalled. Then they branched out into hardships they had faced, successes and failures, hopes and ambitions.

Something quite remarkable began to happen. As these people looked back at their lives, which had seemed insignificant at first, they began to appreciate how rich they had actually been. One said, "For the first time, I took the time and the courage to look at my past and found it rewarding. I was surprised at the strength with which I was meeting situations and crises."[1] It was true that their lives had consisted of a multiplicity of small things, but they were good, valuable lives nonetheless. Many of these seniors ended the course with a heightened self-esteem and a good feeling about the way their years had unfolded.

The Christmas after I read about this experience, I gave my mother-in-law a notebook, a pen, a copy of the original article, and encouraged her to give it a try. Like the others, she too had some misgivings but promised that she would begin. Memories of childhood Christmases came first. Writing about those opened up other subjects and many conversations. Once she told us about the accidents she remembered from her days as a girl on the farm: the runaway team, the gunshot wound, the broken leg from a game of "chicken," and Uncle John's bloody cut from a plow (his young sisters, the only ones home at the time, finally hung him upside down to stop the bleeding). I encouraged her to write an entire chapter called "Close Calls." Reminiscences of life on the farm in the early part of this century provided plenty of those.

Here again, Sister Enid, was that multiplicity of merely small events, not the stuff of cover stories or television miniseries. They may not have counted for much on the total world scene, but they added up to a rich, colorful story and a valuable life. Relationships especially stood out as profoundly important and enduring.

Your pungent words came back to me in a very different way as I was reading about people's "near-death experiences." A few years ago these mysterious occurrences were much in the news, and many books on the subject were published. We learned of people who appeared to have died but who had actually passed briefly into a place of light and peace from which they returned. They told of floating up and viewing their "dead" bodies below, whether it was on the operating table or the battlefield. Many were very reluctant to come back to this world; in fact, they were angry at doctors for "saving" them. I heard two speakers tell their own story of such experiences, and I read studies set up to verify the authenticity of such events. Recently I went back to some of those books again, and I was struck with two things that I think you might find interesting.

Certain features were identical in all near-death experiences, even though the specific circumstances varied widely. All returnees spoke of a "life review," during which they saw their whole life clearly, even the most minor incidents. Then, with the aid of a "Being of Light," they judged themselves. What I found so intriguing was their realization that the big, prestigious events that had mattered the most in this world did not count for much in the life review. Degrees earned, awards won, financial success, career achievements—these were not even on the list. Instead, love was the sole standard by which people were judged. It was one's loving actions that counted—and not just great heroic feats either. The smallest acts of compassion, consideration for others, thoughtfulness, the sort of things a person might do without even thinking—these were valuable. What people most regretted was the failure to do those same small acts of love, the missed opportunities for the kind word or pat on the back. There it was again, that multiplicity of small events and how important they are—"staggering" for sure.

As I read these accounts, Sister Enid, I saw another quality in them that I was sure you, as a philosophy professor, would find appealing: the discovery that after love, the most important thing is knowledge. These were reported as being the only two things a person can take into the next life. I recall your putting those two ideas together in class, saying that "we cannot love what we do not know." It was amusing to read how many people had become avid readers after returning from the place of light. One man confessed that he previously had nothing but contempt for scholars and teachers, thought they were "lazy, doing nothing of any practical value and living off the fat of the land." While he was working long hours seven days a week, they were doing research and writing books "that didn't have a thing to do with anything real." After the Being of Light, whom he identified as Christ, had showed him the value of knowledge, he no longer scorned the professors and their work. Now he reads everything he can get his hands on and is delighted to have the time for learning![2]

A friend of mine once said she hoped that in heaven we could continue to study and learn new things. If she accepts those near-death stories, I have good news for her. Returnees say that learning goes on forever; some "describe an entire realm of the afterlife that is set aside for the passionate pursuit of knowledge." Doesn't that sound great? I imagine you'd be happy to spend a few eons there.

At this point, Sister Enid, you are either writing me off as loony or you are as intrigued as I am. Maybe I lean toward believing these reports because they are so compatible with what we have professed in the Creed all our lives about "the communion of saints, the forgiveness of sins, the resurrection of the body and life everlasting." In the working out of those big truths, the multiplicity of small events apparently plays an important part.

At the risk of belaboring the point, I want to mention just one more case. Some years ago our pastor was given a diary kept by a man in the late nineteenth century, a farmer near a small town in Wisconsin. For a week or two at daily Mass, Father's homily consisted of a passage from this diary and some insights to be gained from it. These were accounts of the plain lives of simple, hard-working people. No mention here of the gross national product or political currents or international treaties or glittering celebrities. We heard instead of bitter winter weather, trouble with the cattle, deaths in the community, family gatherings, hitching up the team to drive to Mass, people moving away, others coming—the same old multiplicity of small events. Somehow it was very moving, though, and for two weeks we felt a kinship with that family of one hundred years ago.

Surely it must be the Incarnation that makes the multiplicity of such small things in life so significant. Once God chose to take on all the baggage of our human flesh and earthly life—in Christ—how could any human event ever be trivial? If we really believe what we profess—that God actually dwells within us—we can see how even the smallest event can have enormous significance. Our world itself has become sacred because this is where God came to walk with us. It might be a good idea for each household to hang a large colored picture of that view of earth sent from the moon by the astronauts—that lovely blue-green globe we call home. It could be a constant reminder that this is a redeemed planet, a sacred world, and what goes on here is infinitely important.

Like the members of that autobiography class, most of us do not see our lives as anything special. No history-changing decisions, we think. Nothing important enough for posterity to notice. No mention in the *Guinness Book of Records*. But the frequency with which your words have come to mind over many years, Sister Enid, has taught me how priceless even small events and quiet lives are.

People who think that their lives are trivial ought to make a list of every person to whom they have ever given a helping hand, a cheery word, a pat on the back, a look of encouragement, a letter, a visit, a gift, a call, good advice, a meal, a band-aid, a ride, a shoulder to cry on, a smile, a hug—that multiplicity of small events which have eternal value. If they had not acted, the world would be lacking that much love. What could be more important than that?

We could also take one man's suggestion that instead of examining our conscience every night to pinpoint all the things we did wrong, we might review the day with an eye for the things we did right. We could include the small kindnesses shown us by others too. Maybe such a practice would keep us alert to the importance of the loving act, the gracious gesture.

I hope you don't find it insulting, Sister Enid, that instead of writing about some great life-changing truth learned in your philosophy class, I bring up that odd little exchange in your office. (I would like to think that those great truths, though not recalled specifically, did soak in and make a difference in my life.) It's just that the other sentence has been so much fun to quote—delightful, too, to see how many times it made sense. Who knows, perhaps in its own weird way that little sentence expressed as profound a truth as some of the others we learned.

Isn't memory amazing? Here it is decades since the days of the "I Am," the "anemone," and the "multiplicity of events," and they are as fresh in my mind today as when they were spoken. How could either of us have predicted then the longevity of such small things? It is, just as you said, truly "staggering." So, Sister Enid, I send my belated thanks.

An old student still learning,

Pat Gits Opatz

To Hermann the Cripple

"Pain Is Not Unhappiness"

Dear Hermann,

If you lived in my day instead of the eleventh century, people would not dare call you Hermann the Cripple. We have become more sensitive about such offensive nicknames—at least we like to think so. Not in your day, though. In reading a bit of history from your period, I came across men called Charles the Bald, Balbulus the Stammerer, Labeo the Thick-Lipped, Charles the Fat, and yet another Charles known as the Simple. It's nice to see that there were some complimentary labels, too, for the lucky ones like Louis the Pious, Robert the Strong, and Hugh the Great.

The sensitivity I speak of was a long time coming, however. One of our neighbors when I was growing up, a man my father worked with, was always called Dummy, because he was deaf and mute. I'm mortified now to recall that no one thought anything of it and probably couldn't have told you the man's real name. It was the same with Crazy Chris and Handbag Hannah— never known (to us youngsters, anyway) by any other names. I'm appalled to think of it now and wonder how they felt about their labels or if they knew of them. Maybe it was the same with you—you got used to being called Hermann the Cripple.

Your name came into my thoughts very unexpectedly recently and prompted this letter. Here's how it happened. In 1951 we gave my dad a copy of Sheed & Ward's *The Guest-Room Book,* a delightful mix of readings designed for the pleasure of one's house guests. Here, for the first time, I read your story as told by C. C. Martindale, S.J.[1] The book came back to us some years later, and except for an occasional dusting it was forgotten among others on the shelves. Until this summer.

It was a day when I was feeling very sorry for myself, wondering if I would ever be rid of the walker and the canes, the limping and the struggle to walk normally, the hurting. I began to fear that this might be a permanent condition, not merely a phase to be endured before being well again. Oh my, I was really wallowing in it, Hermann, getting moodier by the minute. A real pity party. And *that's* when I suddenly remembered you and your amazing story. It felt like a rap on the knuckles from God to quit griping. Back I went to read your story again.

You were born in 1013 to a family that could boast of "gorgeous families . . . noblemen, crusaders, and great prelates." We don't remember a single one of them, however, only you, a child the author calls "horribly deformed" and "hideously distorted." You were not able to stand or walk, could barely sit, and your fingers were so twisted and frail you could barely hold on to things, much less write. That wasn't all. Because of your malformed mouth and palate, people could hardly understand you. Maybe that was one of many reasons you were also regarded as mentally deficient.

In our more "enlightened" day, I regret to say, your secret would have been found out while you were still in the womb, and your parents would have been given the choice to abort you immediately. We would hear pious explanations about the poor quality of life you would have had to endure. When we add to your sad story the fact that you were one of fifteen children— well! How could there be any other choice but to quietly put you, poor "defective freak," out of your misery?

I love what the author says next regarding your parents' choice: "What did these people, skulking in the murk of the 'Dark Ages' (as we have the steely nerve to call them) do? They sent him to a monastery, and they prayed." You went to Reichenau when you were seven years old.

Historians tell us that monasteries in those days were like universities, storehouses of great works of literature, science, art, and music from both the East and the West. Reichenau was outstanding for its scholars, musicians, and artists, as well as its vast library. In this atmosphere you grew up. And you, the boy with the twisted body who could only stammer, began to flourish. We know today how healing and nurturing tender, loving care is, how essential for children's healthy development. You must have received that kind of affectionate care in the monastery, just as you had at home. Though you were almost certainly always in pain, you began to study and learn. It seems incredible, but you, who were "never . . . at ease in a chair nor so much as flat in bed, learnt mathematics, Greek, Latin, Arabic, astronomy and music." Not bad for a hideously distorted child with no future.

Not only did you write a treatise on the astrolabe, a scientific instrument of your day, but even more astonishing, with your gnarled fingers you *made* astrolabes, as well as clocks and musical instruments! You also studied and composed music, even wrote a peppery little treatise about the correct way to sing, saying that most singers just sing without thinking, yet "no one can sing properly if his thought is out of harmony with his voice." That piece reveals your modesty and sense of humor, too, as you call your mind "slower than any donkey, yes, than snail." Maybe so, Hermann, but you managed to produce many scholarly works besides the one on music.

I was curious about you and wondered where Father Martindale could have found the tale of such an obscure person. Imagine my surprise to discover that you are not obscure at all. One encyclopedia devotes two-thirds of a page to you and gives you a large share of the credit for Reichenau's renown as a center of learning.[2]

As impressive as this record is, the real reason for my letter is something else. It's your spirit, your attitude, that really bowls me over. Father Martindale quotes from your Latin biography, where you are described as "pleasant, friendly, easy to talk to, always laughing, never criticising, eagerly cheerful." It's no wonder that "everybody" loved you. The encyclopedia article calls you a "noted and remarkably capable teacher," due as much to your "charm and attractiveness of manner" as your "admirable learning." I put this picture next to that of your physical deformity with its limitations, and I am awestruck. It's no wonder that your name came to me on a day I had the nerve to feel sorry for myself. That recollection has been humbling but instructive too.

Since that first moment of truth, your name has surfaced numerous times, sometimes as an insight into an experience, other times as a question, most often as a reminder to quit complaining and count my blessings. It's as if I had made a small needlepoint sampler of the words "Remember Hermann," like those that say "Welcome" or "Peace." But instead of hanging on the wall, this one hangs inside my head and does the reminding interiorly. (Or maybe it's more like a flashing neon sign—when it lights up, I remember you and the burdens you carried with a merry spirit.)

It came to me, for example, in a memory of something my aunt, Sister Marie Louise, said when I visited her in the home for elderly sisters. She told me how forcefully the words "The Body of Christ" impressed her as she heard them spoken again and again to the sisters as each received Communion. Many of these women, once active nurses, teachers, scholars, and housekeepers, were now bent and frail. They walked with the help of canes and walkers, some in wheelchairs. Others were blind, approaching the Eucharist leaning on the arm of a sister able to lead. The words "The Body of Christ," followed by their "Amen," were a powerful testament to what our faith teaches: these frail sisters *were* the Body of Christ. In the Eucharist, Christ humbly takes up residence even in tired, worn-out bodies, and "we become what we eat." I think of you among that number too, Hermann, your distorted body as much a temple of the Holy Spirit as the fittest athletic champion. (As I've often said, some of us are going to appreciate glorified bodies more than others.)

An experience this summer brought you to mind again. In early May I had to start using a wheelchair and then a walker—a temporary situation that lasted much longer than expected. More than once I protested that I would not go to our daughter's wedding this summer, and *certainly* not to my high school class reunion, in a wheelchair. (It was vanity, no doubt, not wanting people I hadn't seen in decades to view me as a disabled person.) But go I did, wheelchair and all. The class reunion was the hardest, but it was also an education, in fact a revelation.

For the first time in my life, I experienced what it's like to be sitting in a wheelchair, having people standing above talking *down* to me. I felt what it was like to see an old friend across the room and not be able simply to walk over and greet her, or to ease into a circle of conversation. First I had to indicate to my ever-patient husband in what direction I needed a push. Classmates were wonderful, going out of their way to be helpful and giving me special attention. I was grateful for their kindness, and at the same time uncomfortable about being perceived as disabled, not independent on my own two feet. I even *felt* different—fragile, not quite all there. In an odd way I felt somewhat detached, as if I were watching everything from a distance. I am certain it affected my behavior in subtle ways, made me more reserved and inhibited than I would normally have been.

For some reason I felt compelled to let people know, in fact to say repeatedly, "This is only temporary," as if that made a difference. When I discovered three classmates for whom a wheelchair is *not* temporary, I decided it was time to keep my mouth shut. In a sense it *was* temporary even for them, I suppose, because they had enjoyed some good years before the disability occurred. For you, however, Hermann, there wasn't any good time: you came into the world crippled and lived your whole life that way. I have fresh appreciation now for anyone who has such a lifelong burden to carry. I am especially in awe of anyone who, like you, does it while remaining "eagerly cheerful . . . always laughing . . . and never criticizing."

If I ever kid myself that I am at the advanced point you reached, accepting "diminishments" with a happy spirit, I will recall my reaction to a television commercial I saw recently. A healthy young woman, explaining why she uses a certain calcium supplement, said, "I don't want to be one of those bent-over old women shuffling along behind her walker." "Good grief," I thought, "she's talking about *me!* Is that how I look to other people?" Once again my "Remember Hermann" light flashed, and I wondered how many times you felt people staring at you, whispering and making judgments. And I marveled again at your cheerful spirit.

Earlier in this letter I mentioned some questions your story brought to mind, especially that joyful attitude. I can't resist asking if there were times when, alone in your cell, you indulged in a little self-pity, broke down and wept, or heaved something across the room in frustration. What kind of struggle did you go through before you could embrace your cross and be the happy person we read about? Was it the little limitations that bothered you the most, the maddening time and effort it took to do even the smallest chores? (And you made clocks!)

I try to imagine what it was like for you in the monastery. I suspect that when you first went there as a boy, you hoped and prayed to be healed and made whole like other boys. Then, as you matured and deepened, I see your prayer changing to one of acceptance and finally even joy. It must have been a struggle at times, though, especially with the nagging pain always there as a reminder.

I like to think that now and then during your years of affliction God blessed you with some special moments of grace, some "mountaintop" experiences to comfort and sustain you. I hope that such insights gave you absolute certainty that you did not walk alone but that Christ walked with you. Maybe it was remembering such holy moments that kept you from becoming bitter or cynical. Apparently you fought your battles in private, for your confreres saw only the beautiful end result. If your faithful friend Berthold saw you in your weaker moments, they were long forgotten by the time he recorded your story.

These days people fighting the depression that often accompanies long-term illness or disability are advised to program certain activities into their lives as therapy. It's important for them to be working on a creative project, to spend time with people who love them and give them a lift, to provide humor and laughter daily. "Therapy" wasn't the buzzword in your day that it is now, but it looks to me as if all those healthful things were in your life in abundance.

You also had an abundance of the most important coping skill of all—prayer and faith in a loving God, nourished with large doses of Scripture reading. You were a monk in a Benedictine house, where the Divine Office and the prayerful reading of Scripture were a regular part of your day. I wonder whether such reading sometimes stirred up strong emotions. For example, at some time or other you must have read, as I did recently, the passage in one of St. Paul's letters where he says, "We are God's work of art." (A different translation says, "We are God's handiwork.") I imagine myself in your shoes, and I know those words would have prompted me to sarcasm (at least until I had mellowed like you), especially the next time I looked in a mirror: "Yeah, some work of art all right." You, however, would have found some gracious way to make light of it, I'm sure. (We could think of you as an *abstract* work of art, perhaps—deep with inner meaning not immediately perceived. Maybe some such thought cheered you and enabled you to take the long view, as one must with any work of art.)

There were other words of St. Paul that you could more readily embrace: "In my own flesh I fill up what is lacking in the sufferings of Christ for the sake of his body the Church," or "Continually we carry about in our bodies the dying of Jesus so that in our bodies the life of Jesus may also be revealed." I suspect that you felt a special kinship with the mysterious suffering servant of Isaiah, wondering why God had also been "pleased to crush you in infirmity." You could take comfort in the servant's final vindication, though, and trust that like him you would finally "see the light in fullness of days."

All such life-out-of-death themes in the Scriptures (the "paschal mystery" we call it today) would have given you reason to hope. Consoling, too, was the belief that suffering need not be meaningless but can have redemptive value. No doubt you "offered up" your suffering as intercessory prayer for others, as people still do. Once when I had to wear a body brace for months, I would offer each day of it as a prayer for a specific person or cause. It was a rich resource that I no longer had once the brace was removed. You carried yours until the day you died.

The most moving part of your story comes in the description of your death. For many days you had been ill and in steady pain. You told your dear friend Berthold (the one who recorded your story for later generations, bless him!) that you would not survive this illness and would be dying soon. At that news he broke down and wept uncontrollably. After a while you "quite indignantly upbraided" your friend and told him not to weep for you. Indeed, you confessed that you were tired of living. Then you asked him to write down a few things for you and ended with this message: "And by remembering daily that you too are to die, prepare yourself with all your energy for the selfsame journey, for, on some day and hour, you know not when, you shall follow me forth—me, your dear, dear friend."

This nearly thousand-year-old advice to prepare for death sounds remarkably similar to two prayer suggestions I have read in the past few months. One has the eye-catching title "Practice Dying." Here we are advised to imagine vividly all the details of our own death—in fact, more than once, in different circumstances. Though it may sound morbid at first and takes courage, especially for that last step into the unknown, it can have great value. Gradually, the author says, one comes to see death as the natural part of life that it is, and the fear of it is erased.[3]

Anthony de Mello bases several imaginative prayer exercises on the subject of one's own death. He, too, says that these are very fruitful, giving us "not only a fresh appreciation of life but also a sense of urgency." They help us to "avoid wastage" in our lives.[4] I doubt that there was much "wastage" in your life, Hermann, when I ponder all you accomplished and all you became in your forty-one years.

As a subtitle for your story, the author uses a quotation: "Pain is not unhappiness." (He cites no author, but I'm certain they're your words. They sound like you.) Coming from you who learned that wisdom firsthand, I think I have to believe it. It's as if you pondered this matter of pain and deformity, made a conscious choice not to let it control you, then fortified your decision with a life of prayer, study, and service. It's not such a hard truth to swallow during the pain-free times, but when the pain returns, it becomes a formidable challenge. I've thought about it a lot and wonder whether I will be able to accept and act on it when I am tested again.

Your words fly in the face of all that our popular culture says about pain. Forgive my perverse sense of humor, but I wonder what the impact would be if your message, "Pain is not un-happiness," were displayed on the TV screen immediately following a bevy of commercials pushing remedies for tension headaches and various other aches and pains. (Don't be fooled by my flip comments, Hermann—I'm as big a coward as the next person when it comes to heavy-duty pain.)

Already your words about pain have been put in my brain-file along with "Remember Hermann," and I find myself thinking of you often. I am hoping that when I am handed another painful cup to drain, recalling you and the way you handled disability with joy will give me heart. You might just hear a prayer winging your way too. That will be me asking your intercession that I might have your attitude at the end. What a blessing to be able to say, as you did, that the things of this world had become wearisome and that "on the other hand, the world to come, that shall not pass, and that eternal life, have become so unspeakably desirable and clear, that I hold all these passing things as light as thistledown."

Becoming reacquainted with you has been blessing for me, Hermann. I am thankful for the nudge that moved me to read your story again and listen to your wise words, as inspiring now as when you said them centuries ago.

With thanks and hope,

Patricia Opatz

P.S. This is a little bit off my main point, Hermann, but I'm curious. In that first story I read, Father Martindale wrote that it was "practically certain" that you had composed the hymn *Salve Regina* with its plainchant melody. The encyclopedia article, however, dated much more recently, said that the hymn had been "incorrectly" attributed to you. But even more recently, in fact in the hymnal I used just last week, I was happily surprised to see a footnote to the song "Hail, Holy Queen," which said "Asc. to Hermannus Contractus"—Latin for Hermann the Cripple. I like to think you did write that lovely melody, because it gives me a small link to you and Reichenau. That hymn is part of my Benedictine background. Instead of welcoming incoming freshmen to

St. Benedict's College with green beanies and hazing, we used to present a glorious pageant retelling the story of the Benedictine tradition through fifteen centuries. Part of that was singing the *Salve Regina* in Latin. Well, it's just one more mystery to unravel when we finally meet. Oh yes, I look forward to meeting your mother too.

To King David, Poet and Singer

Still Good as New

Dear King David,

For this letter to make any sense to you, I must first tell you about a custom we have here. When we wish to honor people who have done outstanding creative work, we present them with awards. (The Academy Awards come to mind.) The recipients invariably accept the award not just for themselves but in the name of many others, fellow workers equally deserving of the honor. That is what I am asking you to do.

You see, this is a fan letter about the Book of Psalms. I realize that you did not write all the psalms, not even all those traditionally attributed to you. But because you did write some and because your name is so closely associated with the whole collection (and also because I don't know the names of any other psalmists), I am hoping that you will accept my thanks for yourself and all those anonymous writers and singers.

As a musician, poet, and passionate believer in God, you represent for me all those people who created the psalms out of the depth of their own experience. You are still recognized today for your musical and poetic talents, as well as your love for the temple and its liturgy, so it seems to me that you are a worthy recipient. It amazes me to think that your life and mine are separated by nearly three thousand years—thirty centuries!—yet the words you wrote often fit me as if they had been composed with me in mind. That is really the gist of this letter. I thought it would please you to know that your psalms are still being prayed and sung today, still expressing fear, hope, anguish, thanks, praise, anger, love—the same as they did for you.

Well, not exactly the same. You won't find me being pursued by bloodthirsty rivals, waging wars, hiding in caves, confronting the same dangers, political intrigues, and temptations that you did. The Goliaths I face are different from yours. But that's precisely what is so wonderful about the psalms: with a few adjustments, changing a word here or there, I find that they express exactly what I am feeling. They speak from my heart just as they did from yours a thousand years before Christ, and for Christ himself in his turn. I would like to tell you about a few of my favorites and the ways I use them.

I realize, as I look over these well-used passages, that my enemies, like yours, have frequently been physical—not assaults from the Philistines or the Ammonites or the Arameans that you faced, but assaults of serious illness and the fear that invariably tags along.

The first time I decided to memorize a psalm, however, came long before any illness. I had read somewhere that memorizing psalms was like planting a seed in the unconscious mind, that in time it would have a noticeable effect even in the way one thinks and speaks. That was an irresistible temptation for a person like me who is fascinated with words. For my first effort I chose Psalm 27. The lines that attracted me originally were these:

> One thing I ask of the Lord,
>   this I seek,
>   to dwell in the house of the Lord
>   all the days of my life.

I chose these lines simply because they have a lovely sound. As time went on, though, and I continued to work on memorizing, other parts of the psalm took on special meaning. You perhaps were referring to the temple when you said that you wanted to live always in the "house of the Lord." I changed that to "*presence* of the Lord," because I thought it would be a wonderful thing to live with an awareness of God's presence always and everywhere.

In the beginning the words "when evildoers come at me to devour my flesh," struck me as rather melodramatic and I paid them scant attention. A few bouts with serious illness changed that, however. I can't think of a more accurate way to describe cancer, can you? At other times the final beautiful lines about waiting for the Lord were most forceful. That's the great thing about memorizing Scripture—new meanings keep unfolding as the circumstances of life change.

One of the things about your psalms that makes them award-winning is their portability. A psalm is like one of those large handbags with a smaller detachable coin purse you can take with you when you don't want to carry the whole thing. I have found numerous one-liners and two-liners that I detach from a psalm and carry with me into my day. Several of those used together once prepared me for some very painful surgery: I combined "When I begin to fear, in you will I trust" with "Your promise is sure" and "The promise of the Lord is fire-tried." Over and over and over I prayed those—with exclamation points! Then I would *remind* the Lord what he had promised to those who trust. (One of your psalms says that those who trust are "enfolded" in God's mercy. I love that idea.) Those short passages were powerful ammunition for me—as good as your spears and sword were for you in many a battle, David.

Though I use many such detachable prayers from the psalms, I will mention just two more here. Embarking on some domestic project, be it bread baking or that nervous first cut into a piece of fabric, I combine two lines from Psalm 90, add two words of my own and come up with a quick, heartfelt petition: "Prosper the work of [my] hands, O Lord! Prosper the work of [my] hands!" (I'm not one of those efficient "measure twice, cut once" craftspeople, and I need to pray both before and during my efforts.) The other, used when I note a "down" mood coming on or when my attitude has been negative, is "Pleasing to [you] be my theme—I will be *glad* in the Lord." Repeating that last half has been especially helpful when I was heading into a dreaded event; I believe it turned things around more than once, because it made me actually try to face it gladly.

In recent decades we have been treated to one of the psalms daily in the Mass, so we are more familiar with them than we used to be. The trouble is that sometimes we move through them so fast, positioned as they are between the two major readings, that we miss the impact of the images. In a small discussion group I belong to, we have found that it pays to stop and take a good look at some of those. As a result, I have come to appreciate what a great poet you were. More than merely colorful and vivid—which they are—your images also tell us much about who God is. Often the God they show me is tender and compassionate.

Take, for instance, the line where you say to God, "My tears are stored in your flask." Just a simple thought, really, but what a picture it creates of gentle affection: God remembers all the tears we have shed, saving them up the way a mother saves and treasures the hair from her baby's first haircut. More than once you ask God, "Incline your ear to me." If we pause to picture that, we see a loving Father bending down to the child, tilting his head, perhaps even cupping his hand around his ear to hear the child's whispers better. In other places you speak of being sheltered in the "shadow of God's wings," of a "God who bears our burdens," who "guards the passageways of death," our "guardian and shade." You even call God our "allotted portion and cup," like a meal set before us for pleasure and nourishment. Then you tell us to "taste and see how good the Lord is." (These words are especially powerful when we think about the Eucharist.) Such images are a great comfort. We are well rewarded if we take the time to visualize and think about each one.

Some of the psalms show quite a different side of God, the powerful side, and they also remind us that you were a warrior-king. It was natural that you should speak of God as a shield, rock, fortress, strength, refuge, stronghold, deliverer. In one wonderful passage you combine these two sides of God:

> . . . power belongs to God,
> and yours, O Lord, is kindness.

In the margin next to that passage, I once wrote, "What a combo!"

I hope this is not too personal a question, David, but how in the world did you get to be so intimate with God that you dared to speak with such boldness? Most of the pray-ers I know could never do that. And I couldn't either if I hadn't read your words first and accepted them as divinely inspired. You tell God to hurry, to wake up. You complain when God doesn't seem to listen. You argue. You even have the nerve to remind God how faithful and virtuous you have been. You scold and complain and express your anger. And that was three thousand years ago! You would think that people of my generation, with all the sacred writings since your time and all the testimonies of experience, would be at least that intimate with God. But I'm not sure we are. Maybe if we spent more time with your psalms, we would be.

But besides your boldness, there is the other extreme of intimacy—the way you speak of "taking delight" in the Lord. How I would like to know what experiences you had that led you to that idea. Was it something that happened when you were a shepherd, spending long nights and days alone with the flocks? Or was it one of those more dramatic times when, as king, you were saved from some fierce enemy?

When I try to think of a time the Lord has delighted me, I invariably think of very little things. Big interventions of God inspire awe. Delight comes with the little surprises—in one case a very tiny event about a very tiny bird. Years ago, on a local radio program, a man would tell interesting details about a different bird each day. Daily he would sign off with a sing-songy "It's nice to have the birds around." I was sweeping the kitchen floor the day he told of the hummingbird, and I murmured partly to God and partly to myself, "You know, Lord, I haven't seen a hummingbird for years. It would be nice to see one again sometime." Would you believe, that very afternoon a hummingbird landed on the clothesline just outside our kitchen window and remained still long enough for me to have a good look. It was a genuine hummingbird too, not one of those insects that looks like one. Hummingbirds don't sit on clotheslines! They hover and whisk and dart around flowers. This one *sat*—well, perched. A line from one of your psalms describes how I felt: "My mouth was filled with laughter." I definitely took delight in the Lord that morning. In Psalm 37 we are told that when we delight in the Lord, "he will grant [us] our heart's requests." I believe it.

Sometimes I take liberties with your psalms. I hope you don't mind. On January 1 for several years in a row, I have taken as a kind of theme for the new year a line from Psalm 116:

> How shall I make return to the Lord
>   for all the good he has done for me?

Periodically I would write it on the top of a journal page to remind myself always to be thankful. The second line of that passage says:

> The cup of salvation I will take up,
>   and I will call upon the name of the Lord.

Two summers ago I heard that psalm sung at an ordination ceremony, and the words were changed from "cup of salvation" to "cup of life." There was something intriguing about that change, and praying it brought some new insights. To take up the cup of life suggests accepting every cup that life brings to your door, the bad with the good, the sweet tasting with the hard to swallow. Drinking it down is a way of showing trust in God.

I have also made use of your Psalm 16 in a way you couldn't have foreseen. For my entire lifetime the Church has used a prayer for the dead that says, "Eternal rest grant unto them, O Lord, and let perpetual light shine upon them." Who composed it and when or just how official it is, I have no idea. I trust I am not offending anyone by confessing that I don't use it much anymore.

Here's the story. A dear friend died this past year, a priest who loved people and activity. He was always learning and trying new things, literally still getting ideas and writing on his deathbed. He didn't want eternal *rest,* I was sure. He wanted eternal *activity* of a heavenly kind, the chance to keep learning and studying and doing wonderful things for the people he left behind. With his chest pains gone and his eyesight restored now, think of what he could do!

Secondly, the idea of having perpetual light shining on me gives me the willies. I know, it would be celestial light, quite wonderful and all that, but I think I would prefer the "shadow of God's wings." I have always enjoyed soft, gray fall skies more than dazzling, sunny ones, and I don't like to think of spending eternity wearing sun glasses. (I hope I am not being irreverent, David.)

And where did I find the perfect solution? In the psalms, of course. Now I pray for my priest friend, and indeed all my deceased friends and family, with some lines from Psalm 16; I ask God to

> . . . show [them] the path to life,
> fullness of joys in your presence,
> the delights at your right hand forever.

Life, joy, delight, God's presence forever. Sounds like heaven to me.

I have one more psalm story to tell you, a use of your inspired words that was unimaginable in your time. There have been numerous things written lately about the way people under general anesthetic or even in a coma are affected by what is said around them. It has been proved that tapes played to them make an impression on the unconscious mind. Facing a recent surgery under general anesthetic gave me a perfect chance to experiment. Getting permission from a dubious surgeon and anesthesiologist was step one. Then I recorded myself praying a number of psalms, along with other prayers and relaxation exercises. My tape and cassette player went with me into surgery, and I stayed "plugged in" to my headset the whole time.

There is no way I can prove that it made any difference, but I can't help thinking that the results would have to be beneficial. What delights me about it is knowing that your three-thousand-year-old psalms were prayed by way of a battery-operated cassette player in a modern state-of-the-art operating room. I thought you might enjoy knowing that.

One quality I do not find in the psalms is a sense of humor. A modern commentator says that your "predominant feature was violence—perhaps no more than was characteristic of [your] age and culture—but scarcely less."[1] That sounds as though you might not react kindly to a joke. Nevertheless, since you have had thirty centuries in eternity to mellow and work out any grievances you may have held, I think I will dare to end this letter with a little humor. Let's just say it's the price you must pay for getting this award:

King David and King Solomon led merry, merry lives,
With many, many lady-friends and many, many wives.
But when old age crept up on them and they were feeling qualms,
King Solomon wrote the Proverbs, and King David wrote the
    Psalms.

Your loyal fan,

Patricia Opatz

To the Reader

On Letter Writing: One Last Word

Dear Reader,

This last letter is for you. I've thought of you often as I wrote the others, wondering what part letters have played in your life, which ones you have tucked away for rereading and savoring as I have. I like to imagine that something in one of my stories might rekindle a good memory for you, maybe inspire you to get out pen and paper and write to an old friend. You might discover two of the same lessons I learned as this book came together. First of all, I came to appreciate for the first time just how important a role letters have played in my life. I also have observed as never before how letters tend to "increase and multiply." Even as I worked on the book, more letter stories kept coming up. Before my final "Sincerely yours," I want you to hear some of them.

As you know, movies and works of fiction come with a disclaimer that the characters and incidents are fictitious and that any resemblance to real people or events is purely coincidental. The opposite is true here. Each one of these letters involves a person who has transmitted life to me in some way. When I write about a letter I've received—from Oletta Wald or Sister Mariella, from Audrey or Barbara, from Father Mulcahy—you may be sure that these are real letters, not something created as a convenient format for a book. The only fictitious letters here are the chapters themselves. Real or imaginary, every letter seemed to produce other letters.

After I had finished the chapter called "The Demon of Depression," I sent a copy to Barbara. I told her I could do one of three things: change her name as I had done for other patients, use her first name but nothing else, or use her full name and give some identifying details. I also needed permission to quote a part of her letter. Her response was immediate and exactly what I expected: "I definitely want you to be specific—because it is important to let people know *real* people get depression and *real* people get help. Depression is *no respecter* of our status. You can use my name and the part from my letter—anything!" She went on to relate some details from our hospital experience that I had forgotten, including the night when the storms were so bad we had to gather in the dining area and couldn't leave for an hour. "For all who suffered panic attacks it was a bad experience." I treasure my unexpected friendship with Barbara, planted in a difficult time and nurtured with letters.

In order to use the "My name is I Am" quotation, I wrote to its author, Helen Mallicoat, in Arizona. She answered promptly and graciously, saying she would be honored to have her passage in the book. She even added a note that if I'd like to hear the story of how the "I Am" message came to be, she would be happy to tell me. I wrote my thanks and said I would indeed like to hear the story, assuming she had a printed card or leaflet ready to mail out. Not so. She sent two full handwritten pages telling not only how she came to write the "I Am" but what had become of it since. I heard the tale of its amazing, circuitous route from her to me (and now to you) by way of a tuna casserole recipe, a newspaper clipping, the Hallmark Card company, and a score of other stops over many years. Besides the ones I listed in the chapter, Helen wrote of other ways her words had been put to use: a hospital gives the "I Am" cards to patients and their guests, a college professor gives them to his students, a school in Australia put it in their yearbook, Alcoholics Anonymous has used it on tapes, and it has been made into a song. She added, "Of course I gave them permission, for whenever the Lord gives us anything, it is for *all*, His Body."

The tale doesn't end there. Again I wrote thanking Helen for her generous response. The letter she wrote next delighted me even more, for she told me that she has been a letter writer since age ten. That means more than seventy years of letter writing! She also reported that a Round-Robin Letter Club she joined in 1948 is still going strong, though its original thirteen members are now down to three. Helen prefers to write in longhand with pen and ink, and estimates she now averages fifty letters a month! I had no idea when I wrote my formal request for permission that it would result in this delightful correspondence with a woman of great faith.

One special recipient of Helen's letters is Jesus; she writes him a letter every single day. That idea touched me and reminded me of reading once that Father Thomas Price, cofounder of Maryknoll, began writing letters almost daily to the Blessed Mother in 1908 and did so until his death. The letters were often written in notebooks, but some were on the backs of envelopes or bits of paper. Faithfully writing such letters daily over a long period must bring rich spiritual rewards, for surely it is a way of praying.

The dailyness of this practice brings to mind another champion letter writer I want to tell you about—Barb Birkeland. During a time of illness and long before we had met, I began receiving notes and cards from Barb—some prayerful, some funny, always uplifting. She wrote hoping that her thoughts would be "felt support" for me, and they were. I learned that Barb was a colleague and good friend of our daughter Ann, and through her was following the progress of my recovery. (Barb and Ann have also been part of a four-person Round Robin for several years.)

In front of me right now is a card I received from Barb when I was at a low point that spring. Included was a large purple kerchief and this list of possible uses:

> Easter basket—fill with M & Ms
> Neckerchief
> Headkerchief
> Handy Kleenex substitute
> Convenient tablecloth for small meals
> "Wearing o'the purple" fashion accessory
> Easy mirror cleaning rag—just add spit
> Easter basket liner—to guarantee no loss of M & Ms

It was typical of the upbeat messages she sent frequently over many months.

That this very busy woman—who didn't even know me—would use her time and imagination to cheer me was enormously consoling. Every time I use that purple kerchief (as a napkin usually) and every time I iron it, I remember Barb.

Many months later we did finally meet over a cup of coffee, along with our connecting link Ann and another friend. Barb told us that day of a letter-writing practice she had begun years before: she and a close friend, living miles apart, agreed to write each other *daily*. Part of the pact was that each would save the letters from the other, to be returned at some future time, thus providing a daily journal of their lives over many years. Putting this chapter together, I wrote to Barb (now in Montana, where she and her husband, both ordained Lutheran ministers, are busy pastors) and asked if she and her friend were still faithful to their agreement.

Indeed they are. She wrote to say that they are well into their twelfth year. "Boxes of Beck letters at one end and Birkeland letters at the other expand month by month. We treasure the privilege and creative outlet of daily connection, know the delays of the postal service intimately, and her husband figured at ten years our investment was approximately $140 a year—which we assess to be cheap therapy!"

Wouldn't it be fun to visit with these two good friends, hear more about the kinds of things they include in their letters and how they fit such a practice into busy lives? Do they carve out a space first thing in the morning or save the daily message till bedtime as a way to sort out the day and lay it to rest? Imagine yourself writing and receiving such daily letters over years. Then imagine receiving that whole collection some day—like having a huge piece of your life neatly arranged in a box. Such faithful letter writing must be not only very healing but also a way of deepening and enriching the friendship of these two women. I can think of a dozen rewards from such a correspondence, not the least of which would be the guarantee of something worthwhile in the mailbox almost every day of the year.

Futurists say that such mail will soon be obsolete, replaced by all manner of electronic communication. The letters I treasure are derided by technology enthusiasts as "snail mail." A recent newspaper series on the coming digital age included the prediction that two hundred years from now people will marvel, "Can you imagine they used to have print? They used to kill all these trees. . . . And if you wanted to send [a person] something on paper, you could send it slowly over something called the mail system, where actually people had to carry it to the houses where it was delivered every day to the house by person."[1] Sounds pretty scornful, doesn't it?

I hope (and believe) that as the digital age comes to dominate, there will be enough romantics and family historians around to ensure the survival of the personal letter, no matter how antiquated it may seem. I can't quite imagine cherishing bundles of faxes or e-mail printouts, tying them with ribbon and lovingly saving them as we do letters. When you hold a letter in your hand, you know that you are literally in touch with the person whose hand moved over that same paper. In the closet across the hall from where I write is a box containing five decades of letters: from my husband to his parents during his Marine years in World War II, from us to each other during college days before we were married, from children and now grandchildren. Also in that box are the letters which inspired this book and which I have been happy to let you read over my shoulder. What could possibly take the place of such letters, I wonder, even in a cybernetic world?

I hope you will be pleased as I was by what Richard Lederer says about letters in his *Miracle of Language*. He quotes William Swanson: "A good letter, in the era of communications satellites and quipping note paper, is something akin to a handmade afghan or a jar of homemade currant preserves: a small act of grace, a hand-wrought gift from one human being to another." Lederer adds, "You invest only the cost of a stamp—and the gracious impulse to open your heart and mind and communicate with a fellow rider on our planet."[2]

Well, fellow riders, that's what I have done, and now I am nearly finished. The only story remaining for me to tell is not strictly about a letter but rather about a book that has become for me as personal as a letter. It is Patricia Livingston's *Lessons of the Heart.* After reading a friend's borrowed copy, I bought one for myself. Since then I have given that book as a gift to at least ten people. I've read it so many times that I take the liberty of calling the author Pat, as if I knew her well. Her book is real and wise and goes straight to the heart.

In her last chapter Pat Livingston encourages her readers to tell their own stories as she has done: "I wish I could hear your songs and stories, the things that make you laugh. I wish I knew what gives you hope. Perhaps someday you'll pass it on to me."[3] Although I didn't realize it when I began, I believe that's what I have done in this book, at least in small part. One of my hopes for the questions provided at the end is that they will stir up *your* memories and stories too. I like to imagine you with friends or a small discussion group where you can share and appreciate these bits of your life journey. Like the other Pat, I encourage you to do that—in letters, in journals, in scribbled remembrances, in conversation.

Remember, you are a letter that God has written to the world—not a form letter, not part of a bulk mailing, not fourth class or pre-sorted—but unique and special. Only you can tell the story God sent you to tell.

Sincerely yours,

Patricia Opatz

Notes

The Letter to St. Paul

1. Henry Wansbrough, ed., *The New Jerusalem Bible* (New York: Doubleday, 1984) 1852.
2. Pope John Paul I, *Illustrissimi* (Boston: Little, Brown and Co., 1978) 122.

The Letter to Audrey

1. Audrey Mettel Fixmer, after raising their large family with husband Bob, went on to become a teacher, speaker, and writer. She describes herself as "a humorist with opinions," and last year published her first book, *Grand Mom: Growing Old Gracefully and Other Likely Stories.*

The Letter to Worried Parents

1. Anthony de Mello, *Sadhana, A Way to God* (New York: Image Books, 1984) 140.

The Letter to Pope Gregory

1. R. D. Weakland, "Gregorian Chant," *New Catholic Encyclopedia,* 6:757.
2. Interview in *USA Weekend* (October 8–10, 1993) 5.

The Letter to W. Timothy Gallwey

1. W. Timothy Gallwey, *Inner Tennis: Playing the Game* (New York: Random House, 1976).
2. Ibid., 57.
3. Ibid., 58.
4. Ibid., 167.

The Letter to Father Mulcahy

1. Morton Kelsey, *The Other Side of Silence* (New York: Paulist Press, 1976) 1.
2. Ibid., 2–3.
3. Anthony de Mello, *Sadhana, A Way to God,* 85–87.
4. Ibid., 65.
5. Morton Kelsey, *Other Side of Silence,* 61.

The Letter to Baby Boomers

1. Barbara Kantrowitz, "Search for the Sacred," *Newsweek* (November 28, 1994) 52–55.
2. Pope John Paul II, *Crossing the Threshold of Hope* (New York: Alfred A. Knopf, 1994) 24.

The Letter to the Third Servant

1. Maya Angelou, *Wouldn't Take Nothing for My Journey Now* (New York: Random House, 1993) 74.

The Letter to Barbara

1. Barbara is the wife of Pastor Mark Brown of the First Church of God in Bertha, Minnesota, and the mother of two daughters. Like other pastors' wives, she serves in many ways: as musician, teacher, caregiver, hostess, chaperone, and friend, to name only a few. She loves what she does, because she says the people of their congregation are "active . . . progressive, and supportive of the pastor's family."
2. M. Scott Peck, *Further Along the Road Less Traveled* (New York: Simon & Schuster, 1993) 24.

The Letter to Griselda

1. The short quotations throughout the letter to Griselda are from "The Canterbury Tales" in *The Complete Poetical Works of Geoffrey Chaucer,* trans. John S. P. Tatlock and Percy MacKaye (New York: The Macmillan Co., 1938) 197–217.
2. *A New Catechism* (New York: Herder and Herder, 1972) 299–300.

The Letter to Hallmark

1. Bernie Siegel, M.D., *Love, Medicine and Miracles* (New York: Harper & Row, 1986) 199.

2. Siegel, *Peace, Love and Healing* (New York: Harper & Row, 1989) 193.

3. Ibid.

The Letter to Miss Manners

1. The quotations from Miss Manners' column are from Judith Martin's *Miss Manners Guide to Excruciatingly Correct Behavior* (New York: Warner Books, 1982) and are used by permission.

The Letter to Sister Enid

1. Michael Briley, "How to Write Your Autobiography," *Modern Maturity* (August–September 1978) 25–26.

2. Raymond A. Moody, Jr., M.D., *The Light Beyond* (New York: Bantam Books, 1988) 36.

3. Ibid., 35.

The Letter to Hermann

1. C. C. Martindale, S.J., "Hermann the Cripple," *The Guest-Room Book,* assembled by F. J. Sheed (New York: Sheed & Ward, 1948) 228–231.

2. W. C. Korfmacher, "Hermannus Contractus," *New Catholic Encyclopedia,* 6:1073.

3. Elaine St. James, *Inner Simplicity* (New York: Hyperion, 1995) 117–119.

4. Anthony de Mello, *Sadhana, A Way to God,* 96–98.

The Letter to King David

1. John L. McKenzie, S.J., *Dictionary of the Bible* (New York: The Macmillan Co., 1965) 179.

The Letter to the Reader

1. Peter Leyden, "On the Edge of the Digital Age," *Minneapolis Sunday Tribune* (June 18, 1995) 2T.

2. William Lederer, *The Miracle of Language* (New York: Pocket Books, 1991) 201.

3. Patricia Livingston, *Lessons of the Heart* (Notre Dame, Ind.: Ave Maria Press, 1992) 122.

On Second Thought

Questions for Reflection or Discussion

A. The Letter to St. Paul

1. Read St. Paul's second letter to the Corinthians 3:2-3. In what sense are you a letter Christ has written to the world? Who has "read" you lately? What message do you think they got?

2. Do you have a favorite passage from one of St. Paul's letters? What is there in it that speaks to you?

3. Have you ever received a life-changing letter? One that gave you a lift or insight when you needed one? Have you ever learned later that a letter you wrote had such an effect on someone else?

4. Read any of the following prayer passages from St. Paul's letters: Ephesians 1:17-19 or 3:14-19; Philippians 1:9-10; 1 Thessalonians 3:12-13. Which of these prayers would you find most useful for yourself?

5. St. Paul is generous with thanks. See, for example, Romans 1:8; Philippians 1:3-5; Colossians 1:3-4; 1 Thessalonians 1:2-3. St. Ambrose said, "No duty is more urgent than that of returning thanks." Reflect on times when you received a thank-you that meant a great deal to you. How did you feel when you expected and deserved a thank-you and it didn't come? Do you see any connection between this and your own prayers?

6. St. Paul writes to the Ephesians (4:29): "Say only the good things that [people] need to hear, things that will really help them." What are some of the ways letters can do this?

7. Read Jesus' parable about the last judgment, the sheep and the goats (Matthew 25:31-46). What letters could we write that would meet some of those demands?

B. *The Letter to Mother*

1. Read again what Jesus says about people who gather together (Matthew 18:19-20). Do you belong to any small groups (support, faith sharing, Bible study, or coffee-after-daily-Mass group) that have been a source of help to you? What is it that happens there?

2. Read Sirach 6:14-17. Reflect on the role of friends and family during times of serious sickness or other trouble.

3. We may be shocked to read in Psalm 119:71, "It is good for me that I have been afflicted." Yet Bernie Siegel, a surgeon famous for working with cancer patients, writes that "disease can be considered a gift." Patients have called their disease "a beauty mark, a wake-up call, a challenge and a new beginning." How can this be? What is there about serious illness that could be considered a gift? What good could come from it? How can we relate such an attitude to Good Friday and Easter, the paschal mystery?

4. The Book of Proverbs has a few things to say about an idea very popular today: the mind-body connection (15:13; 15:30; 17:22). In what ways do these words have a very modern ring? Can you give examples from your own experience?

5. As we see in the Gospels, a large part of Jesus' ministry was healing. His was the mind-body kind, where soul and body were both treated. How is the Church ideally suited to do this work?

6. What has been your experience with the healing ministry of the Church? Is there more the Church could be doing in following this aspect of Jesus' work? What, specifically, would you like to see?

7. Have you ever tried the prayer of faith imaging? You might experiment with that and see what you think.

C. *The Letter to Audrey*

1. Look again at the mysterious lines from Scripture below. Reflect on your own life with these words in mind. Can you recognize instances where they proved to be true for you? How might recognizing this truth of "dying and rising" be helpful to you in future times of difficulty? (I've added italics for emphasis.)

> "God makes *all* things work together for the good of those who love him" (Romans 8:28).

> "*Only* goodness and kindness follow me all the days of my life" (Psalm 23:6).

> "*All* the paths of the Lord are kindness and constancy toward those who keep his covenant" (Psalm 25:10).

> "Unless the grain of wheat falls to the earth and dies, it remains just a grain of wheat. But if it dies, it produces much fruit" (John 12:24).

2. Jesus says, "Things are hidden only to be revealed at a later time; they are covered so as to be brought out into the open" (Mark 4:22). Have you had the experience of coming to understand certain events of your life only long afterward? How can such insights help build up one's faith?

3. How important have friends been in your life? What qualities do you think it takes to be a good friend?

4. Jesus also has something to say about friends: "I call you friends, since I have made known to you all that I heard from my Father" (John 15:15). What are some of the things Jesus has made known to us about his Father? Do you think of Jesus as a friend? How has that made a difference to you, in the way you pray, for example?

5. Which passages of Scripture have been especially meaningful for you, helpful in times of trial?

6. What do you think of the idea of looking back through the years and then "taking your life in your arms"? What would be some good ways of doing that?

D. The Letter to Worried Parents

1. Christians are supposed to be optimists, people of hope. In the face of so many younger Catholics no longer practicing the family's traditional faith, on what can we base our hope for the future of the Church?

2. What have you found to be the most effective way to make the Catholic faith appealing to others?

3. Jesus says that he will "draw all" to himself (John 12:32). To "draw" means to pull or attract. In what ways does God pull or attract people? How does God use us to do that drawing; what is our role?

4. St. Paul wrote of Abraham, "Hoping against hope, Abraham believed" (Romans 4:18). That is an odd expression: "hoping against hope." The dictionary says that it means "hoping without reason or justification—against all odds." It certainly paid off for Abraham! In what ways can we use our ancestor Abraham as an inspiration and example? You can find Abraham's story in Genesis, beginning with chapter 15.

5. Jesus says that no one can "snatch" his sheep out of his hand, and "there is no snatching out of" the Father's hand either (John 10:28-29). How can such a promise be a comfort to us? Are there ways of applying it to our own family situations?

6. See Psalm 27:14: "Wait for the Lord with courage. Be stouthearted and wait for the Lord." What kind of courage does it take to wait, to bring up children, to be a Christian?

E. The Letter to Pope St. Gregory

1. What favorite hymns from childhood have stayed in your memory? What is there about them that you still find meaningful? Are there particular phrases that you turn to or use in your prayers?

2. How important is music to your worship, your prayer?

3. Several psalms tell us to "sing a new song to the Lord" (for example, Psalms 33:3; 96:1; 98:1). At what times do you think the Lord would like to hear something "new" from us in our prayers instead of the same old song? More praise, more thanks, more joy?

4. Read Mark 14:26. Heading into his passion and death, Jesus sang hymns of praise. Comment? How does that strike you? What does it tell us about Jesus?

5. Read that famous "word" passage from the Letter to the Hebrews (4:12). Has a passage of Scripture ever struck you in one of those powerful ways, for example, judging your thoughts and reflections? How did you respond?

6. Read Mark 4:26-29, Jesus' parable of the seed that "grows of itself." Apply that story to the effect that faithful, prayerful reading of Scripture has in one's life.

7. Read again the comments of Maya Angelou. Think about what the implications of that might be. Your dinner table, for example, or the place where you pray.

F. The Letter to Timothy Gallwey

1. Read Psalm 118, especially verse 24. What influence do you think it might have on your day if you pondered that line briefly each morning?

2. In chapter 4 of Mark's Gospel, Jesus tells several parables about listening to the Word. What kinds of listeners does he describe? Is there some danger that we might not listen carefully to such parables because they are so familiar? What are some things we can do to prevent that? Can our imagination help?

3. Have you had the experience both of being *truly* heard and *not* being heard at all? What was the difference in the way each made you feel?

4. Choose one small act to do with total presence today—with 100% attention, see, hear, smell, taste, and feel all its qualities. Afterwards, think about how it felt.

5. Imagine treating ordinary tools and utensils as if they were sacred vessels of the altar—and then try it. In what sense are all created things sacred? Can they all tell us something about God if we use them graciously and gratefully?

6. Read the words of Jesus in Matthew's Gospel (6:19-34). How realistic do you think they are? What if we took Jesus at his word? Think of daily ways we can apply what he says here, ways that will show we trust his promises.

7. Now read the "I Am" passage again, and compare it with what Jesus says.

8. Examine that Thai maxim, "Life is so short, we must slow down." Does it make sense to you? Why or why not?

9. In the story of Jesus and the woman with the nard (Mark 14:3-9), what is the difference in the quality of presence they experience compared with that of the other guests?

G. The Letter to Father Mulcahy

1. Most people acquire a list of "code words" over the years that only family members understand. What are yours? Are there ways you could convert some of them into useful prayers by using your imagination?

2. Read Psalm 139:13-14. Then take some quiet time to imagine the precise moment when God brought you into being: one moment you did not exist and the next moment you did. Does this help you appreciate that you are "fearfully, wonderfully made," as the psalm says? Reflect for a while on the extraordinary gift of life, how very personal your creation was.

3. Who taught you to pray? Over the years, have you learned and experimented with new ways of praying? What prayers are most meaningful for you? What part does Scripture play in your praying?

4. How do you think God reacts to our use of intimate language and humor in our prayers? It helps to remember that God is a loving parent. How do loving parents act? How do we keep a balance in our prayer between God as close and intimate and God as Almighty and Most High?

5. What do you think of Father Mulcahy's seminary prayer of imagination? Might you try it yourself sometime?

6. Read any of Jesus' parables, and during your prayer time close your eyes, relax, and use your imagination to play a role in the story or observe what happens—for example, the good Samaritan (Luke 10:30-37); the rich man and Lazarus (Luke 16:19-31); the Pharisee and the tax collector (Luke 18:9-14); the prodigal son (Luke 15:11-31).

Or do the same thing using events from Jesus' life—for example, a healing (Matthew 9:1-7; Luke 13:10-17; or Luke 17:11-19); calming the storm (Matthew 8:23-27); the multiplication of loaves (Matthew 15:32-39); the entry into Jerusalem (Luke 19:28-40).

7. Some of the most imaginative—and intimate—language in Scripture is found in the psalms. What new insights arise when you take time to imagine God as rock, shepherd, shield, allotted portion and cup? What do these other passages from the psalms tell you about God:

> "I have waited, waited for the Lord, and he stooped toward me and heard my cry" (Psalm 40:2-4).

> "In the shadow of your wings I take refuge, till harm pass by" (Psalm 57:2).

> "Incline your ear to me; in the day when I call" (Psalm 102:3).

8. Have you ever thought of your imagination as one of God's most gracious gifts?

H. *The Letter to Catholic Baby Boomers*

1. What practices and traditions of the Church have you found most valuable, most comforting?

2. What practices do you think the Church should do more of or do better? Are there any that you could just as well do without?

3. At a time of crisis in your life, how has the practice of your faith been of help to you?

4. St. Paul writes that we should use "prayers and petitions of every sort" (Ephesians 6:18). What prayers of the Church are most meaningful for you?

5. At what times have you best had a sense of real community in the Church?

6. What do you think is the best approach to take in talking to baby boomers who are shopping around for a spirituality,

a meaning in life? Are we conveying the joy of our faith as John suggests in his first letter? (1 John 1:4)?

7. Picture your own deathbed. If you could plan it yourself, what would you arrange? Who would be there? What prayers would you request?

8. One image of the Church is a house of prayer. What is your favorite image of the Church?

9. How does the Church best communicate God's love for all?

I. The Letter to the Third Servant

1. Read the parable of the silver pieces in Matthew's Gospel (25:14-30). Which of the characters can you most easily identify with? What challenges have you faced that tempted you to act like Murphy?

2. Murphy's imagination made a coward of him. How might he have used his imagination constructively, positively? How can we?

3. In explaining the parable of the sower (Luke 8:4-15), Jesus says that "the seed on good ground are those who hear the word in a spirit of openness." How would you characterize someone with a spirit of openness? Who can you think of from the Gospels who showed that openness, who was willing to take a chance and trust Christ? Compare the Gerasenes of Luke 8:37 with the Samaritans of John 4:40.

4. How would you rate yourself on openness to change, to new ideas, people, experiences? What about new ways to pray or nourish your spiritual life?

5. What do you see as the connection between openness and courage, between openness and trust? See Psalm 56:3-4; would this be a good prayer for times when we are afraid?

6. Do you think that we sometimes miss out on some of God's gifts because we are too careful, too stuck in our comfortable patterns?

7. Is there such a thing as being too open-minded? (Someone once said that we don't want to be so broad-minded that we become flat-headed.)

8. How can we discover and encourage people's gifts and talents, including our own?

9. Read Luke 13:34, where Jesus speaks to the city of Jerusalem: "How often have I wanted to gather your children together as a mother bird collects her young under her wings, and you refused me!" In what ways do we sometimes "refuse" Jesus' tender invitation by being closed?

10. In his second letter to the Corinthians (9:6), St. Paul says, "He who sows sparingly will reap sparingly, and he who sows bountifully will reap bountifully." How does this apply to our willingness to take a chance, to risk?

11. Think of some small ways you might take the risk and try something new during the coming week: use a fresh way to pray (silence, the psalms, singing); find a kind word to say about someone you don't like—and say it; say yes where you usually say no; leave some loose ends to make room for the Holy Spirit's creativity.

J. The Letter to Barbara

1. Recall a time when, because of some suffering, you were unable to pray. How did you deal with that? What helped you to get through it?

2. Do you agree or disagree with the notion that it's all right to tell God our deepest feelings, including anger? Does it help to remember that God knows our innermost thoughts anyway? See the first six verses of Psalm 139: God "understands my thoughts from afar" and knows what I am thinking "even before a word is on my tongue." Discuss this passage as it relates to being open and frank in our prayers, no matter what we are feeling.

3. Read what St. Paul writes to the Romans (8:26-27) about the Spirit praying in us. How might this be a comfort at times when we find it impossible to pray?

4. Have you had the experience of discovering after some trial or suffering that you were able to help someone else going through the same thing? How did you make yourself available and share your experience?

5. Read Hebrews 4:15-16. Jesus understands perfectly what is going on in us when we suffer. See also how the Gospel writers describe Jesus in Gethsemane: he is "filled with fear and distress," his "heart nearly broken with sorrow," feeling "terror and anguish." How might meditating on this scene give us encouragement, especially if we keep in mind what happened Easter morning?

6. Comment on the idea that everything that happens to us is designed to teach us holiness. What Scripture passages, especially Jesus' teachings, would support that view?

7. Reflect on Joseph's words to his brothers, especially his summing up: "Even though you meant harm to me, God meant it for good, to achieve his present end. . . ." Have there been times when you were able to take the long view and make sense of something that happened in your life?

8. Read again the entire Serenity Prayer. How would it work for you as a rule of life? What lines speak most powerfully to you?

K. The Letter to Griselda

1. In his letter to the Romans (15:4), St. Paul writes that "everything written before our time was written for our instruction, that we might derive hope from the lessons of patience and the words of encouragement in the Scriptures." Recall some of those lessons of patience from the Scriptures (like Abraham and Sarah, Joseph in Egypt, Moses). In what way can we derive hope from them?

2. Recall some events from your own life that called for patience and words of encouragement. Have you learned any lessons and derived any hope from them?

3. In Isaiah 30:15 we read: "By waiting and by calm you shall be saved, in quiet and in trust your strength lies." What times in your life have you been in some way saved by calm waiting, in which your strength lay in patience?

4. Psalm 107 suggests that the wise person is able to look back over the events of his or her life and see the hand of the Lord in them. If you were to write down the critical events of

your life, would you be able to discern the ways that God was with you and brought you safely through? How might such an exercise help you have more patience in future trials?

5. Do you know any Griseldas personally? What do you tell someone who is bearing terrible injustices patiently rather than working to change them? Which would be more difficult: the bearing patiently or the work for justice? Is there such a thing as too much patience?

6. Listed among the traditional spiritual works of mercy are such things as instructing the ignorant, counseling the doubtful, comforting the sorrowful, admonishing the sinner, and bearing wrongs patiently. The others are all ways of going out in service to others, but bearing wrongs patiently is an interior thing. In what ways do you think bearing wrongs patiently could be a work of mercy?

7. Look again at that final description of patience. Think about some of its specific details and where you might apply them to real life situations.

L. *The Letter to the Grandchildren*

1. Jesus speaks of angels in the Gospel of Matthew (18:10), suggesting two of their roles: adoring God and watching over God's children. How do you view your angel's part in your life?

2. A long passage in Hebrews (1:1-14, especially verse 14), says that angels are sent to serve "those who are to inherit salvation." That's you and me. How do you think angels do that? Have you had any personal experience of having been served by an angel? Do you suspect that angels still come disguised as ordinary people, as they did in the Bible?

3. Psalm 34:8 says, "The angel of the Lord encamps around those who fear him, and delivers them." How do you envision that word "encamps"? Do you find it comforting? What does it tell us about God's concern for us?

4. The psalms give us good examples of pray-ers speaking to God freely, boldly. See Psalms 40:14; 44:24; 69:18; 70:6. How comfortable would you be telling God to "Hurry up!" or "Wake up!" as the psalmist does? How outspoken are you with God?

5. The prophet Jeremiah gives us a good example of speaking freely to God. He says, "You would be in the right, O Lord, if I should dispute with you; even so, I must discuss the case with you" (Jeremiah 12:1). Wouldn't this be a great way to approach God over a difficult situation?

6. See Isaiah 62:4 for a passage which says that God takes delight in his people. When do you think we most delight God? See Psalm 37:4 about *our* taking delight in *God*. How do you interpret that in your life, in your prayer? How and when do we delight in God? When does God "turn us on"? What about those times when there *is* no delight at all and God seems far away? How do we pray then?

7. Reminisce a bit. Who taught you to pray—and how? When did you start talking to God in a conversational way? What form does most of your prayer take today? When was the last time you tried something new? What was it and how did it work out?

8. How big a part of your prayer life is the thoughtful reading of Scripture? Do you have any favorite passages memorized? Reflect on those and why you chose them as worth learning "by heart." Find a new passage and memorize it for a good carry-along prayer.

M. The Letter to Hallmark

1. Have you had an experience which seemed totally bad at the time but which actually contained a blessing? How long afterward did you begin to see that? Was knowing that any help to you when the next trial came?

2. How do you react when an unappealing "gift" is delivered to your door?

3. Does the idea of "disease as a gift" seem preposterous to you? How has life-threatening illness affected people in different ways?

4. Think of some of the people Jesus healed, for example the ten men with leprosy (Luke 17:11-17); the blind men of Jericho (Matthew 20:29-34); the man possessed by demons (Luke 8:26-35). They all met Jesus face to face and experienced

a miraculous healing, changing their lives forever. Do you think any of them might have said later, like Bob Fosse, "Thank God I was a leper," or "Thank God I was blind"? Why?

5. In the Gospels, it appears that nothing pleases Jesus more than people who trust. See, for example, Mark's account of the woman with the hemorrhage (5:25-34); the Canaanite woman (Matthew 15:21-28); the centurion and his servant (Matthew 8:5-13). What can we learn from them?

6. Jesus says in another context, "Things are hidden only to be revealed at a later time; they are covered so as to be brought out into the open (Mark 4:22-23). How might we apply this idea to the mysterious suffering that comes into our lives?

7. Paul writes to the Romans (8:31), "If God is for us, who can be against us?" See what he adds in verses 38-39. What trials in our own lives could we add to Paul's list? How might our attitude toward unsightly "packages" and our willingness to accept them be influenced by truly believing this passage?

N. The Letter to Miss Manners

1. What are some specific ways in which good manners can be an expression of the command to "love one another"?

2. In Luke 14:12-14 we read Jesus' plan for a dinner party. How practical does it sound to you? Are there some people who do practice it literally? Who are they? What are some realistic ways in which we might best adapt his plan and use it in our homes and parishes?

3. An exchange from Miss Manners' book:

DEAR MISS MANNERS:

Do you have any guidelines that will help me to feel correct in all situations?

GENTLE READER:

Yes, two of which were given to her by her Uncle Henry when Miss Manners was a mere slip of a girl. They have served her well in all the vicissitudes of life ever since. They are:

1. Don't.

2. Be sure not to forget to.

Of course, this is Miss Manners at her tongue-in-cheek best. But isn't it also what Jesus did in his teaching? Reading through one of the Gospels, decide which of his lessons would fit under each of these rules. Are they good rules? Do they make sense to you?

4. Following are some of the situations Miss Manners covers in her book. Based on what you know of Jesus' teaching, decide what his advice would be in those same situations. Why do you think so? Is there evidence in Scripture, things Jesus either said or did, which illustrate that view?

> (1) gossip; (2) boasting; (3) eavesdropping; (4) speaking to children; (5) holding a grudge; (6) tasteless or bigoted jokes; (7) visiting the sick (Miss Manners is vehement about not staying longer than twenty minutes in most cases); (8) the relationship between employer and employee; (9) complaining.

5. Read again what both Jesus and Miss Manners say about responding to injury or rudeness. Recall times when you were insulted or treated rudely. How did you handle it? What methods did you find that worked for you better than others? How might prayer be a help?

6. What do you think of Belloc's words that "The grace of God is in courtesy"?

O. The Letter to Mrs. O'Meara

1. Moses considered himself a man without talent, but God had other ideas. Read Exodus 4:10-17. What can we learn from this episode about volunteering or accepting a challenge? What role does God play, what role do fellow workers play?

2. Several major prophets argued against a mission that God wanted them to do (see Isaiah 6:5-8 and Jeremiah 1:4-8). What finally makes the difference? Could that give us the courage we need to try some challenging projects we may not feel ready for?

3. In Acts 4:13 we see all the important religious leaders looking down on Peter and John as "uneducated men of no standing" and wondering how lowly "men of [their] stripe" (verse 7) could be speaking with such power. What's the answer?

4. How do you interpret the comment that "anything worth doing is worth doing poorly"? Do you see some practical wisdom in it? What happens if people volunteer only for the things at which they feel they are experts?

5. Sometimes people are not even aware of their gifts or strengths. What are some of the ways we can bring them out and encourage them?

6. Read Acts 6:1-6. Note that these were "deeply spiritual and prudent" men who did not look down on being chosen and prayed over just to "wait on table." Are there any lessons to be learned here?

7. Different periods in our life may call forth different gifts. What gifts or talents are you using now that you didn't use earlier in your life? And vice versa?

8. Have you ever taken the risk and attempted to do a task for which you didn't feel quite adequate? Did you put it in God's hands first? What happened?

9. Reflect on the words in 1 Peter 4:8-10, especially about "putting your gifts at the service of one another, each in the measure [you] have received."

P. The Letter to the Woman at the Well

1. Read the story of Jesus and the Samaritan woman at the well in John's Gospel (4:4-42). Look at all the words spoken by the woman. What kind of impression does she make on you? Why do you think Jesus strikes up a conversation with her?

2. What other life-changing meetings have you read about in Scripture, considering both the Old and New Testaments?

3. Have you ever experienced such a watershed moment, or turning point, in your life? What happened? How did it change you?

4. Writing this letter was a revelation to me of how an imaginary letter can be a good lead-in to prayer. Can you think of any characters in the Bible you have been curious about and would like to know better? Why not write them a letter as I have done here? You may be pleasantly surprised at what you discover.

5. Water is an important element in this story, as it is in many other events of Jesus' life. Recall as many of those events as you can in which Jesus used water or spoke of it. What are some of the instances in your own life in which water plays a part? Why is it a good symbol for life?

6. The woman at the well was ready and open for her encounter with Jesus. What things can we do to be open and ready for a movement of grace into our lives?

7. Think about these words of Meister Eckhart: "Be prepared at all times for the gifts of God, and be ready always for new ones. For God is a thousand times more ready to give than we are to receive."

Q. *The Letter to Sister Enid*

1. What words or phrases heard long ago, perhaps from a parent or teacher, have turned out to be very significant for you, have grown in meaning over the years? In what ways have they affected your life?

2. Jesus compares the kingdom of God to a mustard seed and to yeast (Matthew 13:31-33), both dynamic things that start very small, then grow to be huge. What small, seemingly trivial kindnesses have turned out to be important to you? What small things have you done for someone else or said to them that made a bigger difference than you would have thought possible? In what ways do you think loving acts can be contagious?

3. Read what St. Paul writes of a time when he was "restless and exhausted . . . under all kinds of stress" (2 Corinthians 7:5-7). How did God "give heart" to him? How has God used your friends or family members to "give you heart" when you were "low in spirit"? How have you been able to do this for others? Did it require great efforts, or were small acts and words effective?

4. Read St. Paul's classic description of love in 1 Corinthians 13:4-13. Can you see how this might be confirmed by returnees' accounts of their near-death experiences? Do you find these reports credible? Why or why not?

5. Paul writes that each of us is a temple of the Holy Spirit (1 Corinthians 3:16-17); Jesus says that God will come and dwell

in us (John 14:20, 23). How do these teachings assure us that even our small deeds and words can be eternally important?

6. In his book *Illustrissimi* (151–152), Pope John Paul I tells the story of the Irishman standing in line at the gates of heaven, waiting to be checked in. People ahead of him are being admitted as Jesus reads from the ledger that they have fed the hungry, given drink to the thirsty, sheltered the homeless, etc. The poor man can think of nothing good he has done and fears that he will be rejected. Jesus checks the book and says, "There's not much here. However, you also did something: I was sad, dejected, humiliated; you came, told me some jokes, made me laugh, and restored my courage. Paradise!"

The Pope comments that although it's only a joke, it "underlines the fact that no form of charity should be neglected or underestimated." Has anyone ever helped you with a laugh? How important do you think humor is in the life of the spirit? Note what Reinhold Niebuhr (the man who wrote the Serenity Prayer) said about humor: "Humor is the prelude to faith, and laughter is the beginning of prayer." Comment?

7. List moments or events in your life that you treasure most, the memory of which makes you feel good. Are they big events or a multiplicity of small events?

8. Read the scene of the last judgment (Matthew 25:31-46). In what small, daily ways have you done these things or could do them now? Think also of the traditional corporal and spiritual works of mercy and of the multiplicity of small ways in which they can be performed.

9. The next time you attend Mass, pay special attention to that moment at the offertory when the priest puts the drop of water into the wine. That drop represents us, all that we are and all we have done, "the work of human hands." This is the moment to offer to God the multiplicity of small events that have made up your life that week.

R. *The Letter to Hermann*

1. Try to imagine the story of Hermann and its outcome had he been born in our time. What do you think of his par-

ents' decision to send him to Reichenau? What might be a modern parallel to that choice?

2. Read Ephesians 2:10, where St. Paul writes that "we are truly [God's] handiwork." The word "handiwork" suggests something made by hand, that is, with personal attention and effort. That is how God made us. Do you think of yourself that way and appreciate your uniqueness? How might we grow in appreciation for ourselves—and others—as God's unique works of art?

3. In Colossians 1:24 St. Paul writes, "In my own flesh, I fill up what is lacking in the sufferings of Christ for the sake of his body, the church." This is a power we all have—to use our sufferings for the sake of others in the Body of Christ, for we are all members. As Paul says in another place, "If one member suffers, all the members suffer with it; if one member is honored, all the members share its joy" (1 Corinthians 12:26). Have you found it comforting to know that your pain need not be wasted but can be offered as prayer for someone else? How have you put that truth into action?

4. Similarly, we read, "Continually we carry about in our bodies the dying of Jesus, so that in our bodies the life of Jesus may also be revealed" (2 Corinthians 4:10). Do you think that remembering this would comfort you in your times of pain? Where is Jesus suffering, being crucified again, in the world today?

5. What is your reaction to Hermann's philosophy that "pain is not unhappiness"?

6. Read parts of the suffering servant song of Isaiah (52:13 through 53:12). Which lines might have had special meaning for Hermann, as for anyone seriously disabled?

7. We often hear the expression "the mystery of suffering." Why is suffering regarded as mysterious? What is the Christian answer to the mystery?

8. Suffering makes some people compassionate but makes others bitter. What do you think makes the difference? Where does faith come in? Humor? Creativity? Friendship? Any other helps?

9. Someone once wrote that Jesus, being God, really became "disabled" by becoming man, because of the infinite condescension it required. In that sense, then, all of us are disabled.

How might that thought affect the way we think of and behave toward disabled people?

10. Reflect on Hermann's attitude toward death. What is your own view of death and the life to come? Scripture often pictures heaven as a great banquet. What pictures of heaven do you find yourself imagining?

S. The Letter to King David

1. Which images of God found in the psalms have the most meaning for you?

> God who bears our burdens (Psalm 68:20-21)
> Guardian and shade (Psalm 121)
> Our allotted portion and cup (Psalm 16:5-6)
> Shield, rock, fortress (Psalm 18:2-3)
> Light (Psalm 27:1)
> Shepherd (Psalm 23:1-4)
> Host (Psalm 23:5-6)

What is your own image of God? How has it varied at different times in your life?

2. Do you have a favorite psalm or passage from a psalm? What made it appealing to you? In what circumstances do you use it?

3. Reflect on the boldness of the psalmist. For examples, see Psalms 10:1; 13:2-4; 44:24-27. When you are under stress, how do you speak to God? What prayers do you turn to? How might the psalms teach us to be more open and frank with God?

4. Almost all the psalms (even the ones where the psalmist feels abandoned or frustrated), end in praise. One dramatic instance of this is the "Good Friday" psalm, Psalm 22. What part does praise play in your prayer? Do you think that the psalms could be a help here? See Psalm 50:14-15, 23 for some encouraging words about the prayer of praise.

5. The psalmist remembers and learns from past experience (see Psalms 77 and 78, for example). How do you think it can be a help to remember the times in the past when God has answered your prayer?

6. When do you most clearly experience God's presence?

7. There is much talk of "enemies" in the psalms, usually literal warring enemies. Who or what do you consider the enemies in your life? How do you deal with them in prayer?

8. Compare the psalmist's attitude toward enemies (Psalms 11:5-6; 18:40-43; 35:4-6) with the teaching of Jesus (Matthew 5:38-48).